More Dubious [illegible] Finebaum, the Sports Commentator Everyone Loves to Hate . . .

"Paul Finebaum is a nondescript, adenoidal, weasel-eyed, narrow-chested, stoop-shouldered, repulsive creature with all the outward appearance of a cretin ... . I've read a lot of books in my time but this isn't one of them."

—**Tommy Charles**, Birmingham's longest-running talk-show host.

"Paul Finebaum offers the most unique sports commentary of anyone in the football-crazy Deep South. He is the most willing of any columnist to speak his mind."

—**Dick Weiss**, *New York Daily News*

"When I was told Finebaum's book was going to be his best work, I expected a very small book."

—**David Lamm**, television and radio host in Jacksonville, Florida

"It doesn't bother me that he calls me uppity."

—**Donald Watkins**, attorney for Eric Ramsey

"Paul doesn't need a caddy to go look for his golf balls. He needs a troop of Boy Scouts."

—**Chi Chi Rodriguez**

"Paul Finebaum has done more to change the face of sports journalism in the state of Alabama than any other individual."

—**David Housel**, Athletic Director, Auburn University

"You haven't really made it until you've been Finebaumed."

—**David Climer**, *The Tennessean*

"I expect him to be abusive. I respect the fact he gets on everybody's case. What I respect the most is that he has never deceived me."

—**Pat Dye**, former Head Football Coach, Auburn University

"In a state where sports—especially football—are treated with reverence, Paul Finebaum has come into the cathedral beating a bass drum. Not many have hummed along but no one can ignore him, either."

—**Cecil Hurt**, Sports Editor, *Tuscaloosa News*

"While I don't often agree with Finebaum, you have to respect him. He is Alabama's finest sports journalist and people around the nation have come to appreciate his talent."

—**Danny Sheridan**, sports analyst for *USA Today* and CNN

"Paul Finebaum is both witty and bright, perhaps too bright for many people most of the time. I have always been surprised that a New York Times *or a* Sports Illustrated *hasn't stolen him away. He is one of the best and brightest in sports reporting today."*

—**Harvey Schiller**, Executive Director United States Olympic Committee, former SEC Commissioner

"I knew Finebaum before Finebaum was cool."

—**Tim Brando**, ESPN

Celebrities Who Declined to Comment on Paul Finebaum for this Book

Bill Clinton

Bill Curry

Bob Lochamy

O. J. Simpson

Eric Ramsey

Gene Jelks

Country Boy Eddie

Reverend Tom Caradine

General Francisco Franco

Don from Downtown (would have commented but we didn't dare get him started).

Worst

THE ~~BEST~~ OF PAUL FINEBAUM

Printed in the United States of America
Published by Crane Hill Publishers
First edition, first printing, September 1994

Cover design by Robin McLendon
Cover illustrations by Ernie Eldredge
Book design by Bob Weathers

Library of Congress Cataloging-in-Publication Data

Finebaum, Paul
The Worst of Paul Finebaum / by Paul Finebaum.
p. cm.
A collection of the author's columns from the *Birmingham Post-Herald*, selected from more than a decade of writing.

ISBN 1-881548-12-0 : $9.95
1. Finebaum, Paul, 1955- . Title
PN4874.F44F44 1994
070.4'4—dc20

94-27886
CIP

Crane Hill Publishers
2923 Crescent Avenue
Birmingham, Alabama 35209

~~THE BEST OF~~ THE *Worst* OF PAUL FINEBAUM

Collected columns from the *Birmingham Post-Herald*

by Paul Finebaum

Published by

CRANE HILL
PUBLISHERS
1994

2923 Crescent Avenue
Birmingham, Alabama 35209

To my mother, Gloria Finebaum, who has always been there for me with love and encouragement, and whose wit and wisdom can be found throughout these pages.

Table of Contents

The Truth About Paul Finebaum

Paul Finebaum has been a sportswriter and columnist for the *Birmingham Post-Herald* since 1980. He has won nearly 100 sportswriting awards, including first place in several national and regional competitions. He has also received the award for the top sports story in Alabama on numerous occasions, and he was named Sports Columnist of the Year in 1993.

Finebaum grew up in Memphis and attended the University of Tennessee. In 1978, he graduated with a degree in political science. He worked at the *Shreveport Journal* before moving to the *Post-Herald*.

Finebaum's articles have appeared in a number of national publications, including *The New York Times, Sport Magazine,* and *The Sporting News*. He has also contributed to stories for *Sports Illustrated*.

When national sports media come to Alabama, Finebaum's office is usually one of the first stops on the circuit. He has been quoted in *Sports Illustrated, Newsweek, People, The Los Angeles Times, The New York Times,* and *USA Today,* as well as *The Washington Post*. He has appeared on ESPN, CNN, and ABC Sports.

Finebaum is also the host of the state's top-rated sports radio show, "Finebaum," which airs on WERC-AM five days a week in Birmingham. He cohosts a Saturday morning show with the legendary John Forney on the same station.

Finebaum has also been involved in various television programs and recently launched a new program, "Six Sports Live with Rick Karle and Paul Finebaum," on WBRC Channel 6 in Birmingham.

Finebaum's pointed wit and merciless humor have gained him a vast following in the Southeast and around the nation.

In 1990 Finebaum married Dr. Linda Hudson, an internist at St. Vincent's Hospital. The couple resides in Birmingham.

Foreword

by Douglas S. Looney

I have known Paul Finebaum for going on two decades. This is, by any definition, cruel and unusual punishment.

Imagine having to deal with him week after week, month after month, season after season, year after year.

I rest my case.

If Finebaum were found dead facedown in a Birmingham drainage ditch, the list of prime suspects would immediately be reduced to 200,000 people.

Once when I was writing a story for *Sports Illustrated* about an old-time, New York-style press agent named Joey Goldstein, a friend of Goldstein's described the way he gets on people's nerves as "the Jewish equivalent of the Chinese water drip."

The same can be said of Paul Finebaum. And often is.

When he lays fingers to computer keyboard to write one of his newspaper columns for the *Birmingham Post-Herald*, Finebaum can be, for sure, cruel and unusual. He also can be vicious, arrogant, rude, capricious, thoughtless, vindictive, unfair or totally off base. Sometimes he's all these things in one column. And these are his good points.

So it's no wonder that for all these reasons, Paul Finebaum is my hero.

When I grow up, I want to be just like Paul Finebaum.

Please let me learn to be as deliciously hateful as he was, for example, in his treatment of former Alabama football coach Ray Perkins. I mean Finebaum got poor ole Ray down, stabbed him, shot him, caned him, and choked him in the public print. Then he took to spitting on him. I have several of his Perkins columns pinned above my bed for inspiration.

There is not a lick of compassion in Finebaum's wicked heart or an ounce of charity in his black soul. Paul Finebaum. My kind of guy.

All of this, of course, is why he has become not only one of the very best sports columnists in the nation (Finebaum writes a three-times-a-week column in the *Post-Herald*) but one of the very best sports talk-show hosts on radio (his daily show is on WERC in Birmingham).

And now, to have this compendium of Finebaum at his worst—which is to say, of course, best—is almost more wonderful than a body can stand. Indeed, it was the sensationally crass Mae West who once said, "Too much of a wonderful thing is wonderful." That's how I feel about this book. My only regret is that it's way too short.

Yet for all the crummy things Finebaum has written about people—and trust me on this, as one who has written my share of crummy things about people—he somehow can retain, or regain, his relationship with them. I mean, come on, these days he plays golf with Ray Perkins.

I rest my case.

There's a reason Finebaum can pull this off: It's because his insights are so keen and sharp and reasoned—in most cases—that even the victims have to admit in the dark of night that he does have a point.

Case in point: In December 1993, I was in Birmingham to cover the SEC championship game between Florida and Alabama. Naturally, Paul and I had gone to dinner; naturally, he made me pay. During the meal, we had been reminiscing about some of the perfectly rotten things he had written about Auburn University over the years. I'm talking full-blown outrageous. He had done all the tractor jokes. And with all of Auburn's past problems with the NCAA, it's no wonder Finebaum once loved it when I said, "Paul, what do you say to an Auburn football player in a three-piece suit?" Finebaum shook his head. I proudly answered, "Will the defendant please rise?" I'm sure he probably stole that one from me when he knew I was out of the country and wouldn't discover the theft. Anyway, as it happened, Auburn was having a big bash at the Sheraton Civic Center to celebrate its unbeaten football season in the first year under coach Terry Bowden.

We dropped by after dinner and suddenly, being with Finebaum, I felt like I was with Michael Jordan, the Beatles, and Presley, all at the same time.

But Paul Finebaum is not only a superstar celebrity. He is, for lack of a better word, adored. It makes no sense to me. People want to talk to him. They besiege him for autographs. They ask him to pose for photographs with them. They name their first-born after him. Everybody wants to be near him. I remember standing off to the side and looking at this spectacle and thinking, "Oh, for Pete's sake."

Understand, too, that while all this was going on for hours, only one person came up to me and asked for my autograph. It was a case of mistaken identity. He thought I was Donald Duck.

Finebaum isn't nearly as good-looking as I am, not nearly as smart, not nearly as rich, and not nearly as good a writer. I'm ignored. He's awash in adulation. Life in no way is fair.

I rest my case.

It is true that Finebaum and I have combined on occasion to write ugly about folks. After Paul had buried Perkins in 1983, I showed up to dance on the grave by writing an SI piece on the same subject. Paul and I went to dinner; naturally I paid. And Finebaum regaled me with stories. I used several in my articles, and at first Finebaum whined that what he had said was off the record. Then he whined he was misquoted. Can you believe it?

Finebaum griping about how somebody writes about him? Please, Paul, we're all adults.

It is true that when I need a truly stupid quote for something I'm writing, I call Paul. Wouldn't you?

Not long ago, I was in Scottsdale, Arizona, writing about a golf tournament. Around 6:30 a.m. I had on my running clothes and was strolling through the hotel lobby to begin my daily jog. Suddenly, up walks Finebaum. I was stunned. It so happened that while I had flown down from my Colorado home on a much-delayed commercial flight and was having to grub around doing the thankless reporting for my story, Finebaum had flown in on somebody's private jet (I'm sure it was loaded with booze and women, although he didn't tell me this for sure) and had spent the previous evening cavorting around Phoenix with the Sun's superstar (and former Auburn player) Charles Barkley. Life in no way is fair.

I rest my case.

Anyway, I loved his "Barkley Does Phoenix" stories. I had tears in my eyes from laughing. Paul gave me $100 on the condition I promise to never repeat what he told me. I promised. However, I can't stand it. Send me a self-addressed, stamped envelope and a cashier's check for $22.16 and I will mail you a 20-page outline of the night's high and low points. Paul's unbelievably wonderful wife, Linda, already has purchased ten copies.

You get the picture. Paul and I have spent a lot of time together—in press boxes where I have explained the game of football to him, in limousines paid for by others, and on his radio show where I have earned him huge ratings. He has never thanked me for anything.

He never will.

Paul Finebaum is a schmuck.

I rest my case.

Hey, get this. When I wrote a book last fall (most of the sensational investigative reporting was done by Don Yaeger) that was a scathing attack on Notre Dame, *Under the Tarnished Dome: How Notre Dame Betrayed Its Ideals For Football Glory*, Finebaum, in one of his columns did go all-out in praise of my work. He decided to do this one night when we were having dinner; naturally I paid. Anyway, the book was particularly hard on Irish coach Lou Holtz. Next thing I know, Finebaum has turned around and written a perfectly gushy, albeit totally untrue column, in full-throated praise of Holtz and Notre Dame. Next, Holtz writes him a letter telling him what a great journalist he is. Clearly, when it comes to being two-faced, Finebaum has retired the trophy.

But, alas, Paul Finebaum is also my friend. Forever. I am stuck with him from here to eternity because he has my unlisted home phone number and he won't give it back.

This book in your hands is a treasure to behold. You're very lucky to have it. Paul hopes you didn't steal it and that you paid full price. However, I will be reviewing this book in *Sports Illustrated*, and I'll be pointing out what an accumulation of crap it is.

Douglas S. Looney, a senior writer at Sports Illustrated, *has been writing for the magazine since 1975. His exposé of Notre Dame,* Under the Tarnished Dome, *reached No. 11 on* The New York Times *bestseller list. He lives in the mountains outside Boulder, Colorado.*

THE ~~BEST~~ Worst OF PAUL FINEBAUM

AUGUST 29, 1983

New era, but only one Bear

In between some rumpled papers and old football schedules in my desk, there was a piece of plain, white paper with a telephone message scribbled on it:

"Coach Bryant returned your call."

Instinctively, I reached for the phone. The message was dated December 11 and a phone call was useless.

It was just a white piece of paper with five words written on it, but it made a dreary gray morning burst alive with memories.

It had been eight months, but my head was filled with the noise of the crowd on that chilly night in Memphis. I remembered shivering on the sidelines watching him being carried off the field with his final victory.

I was too worried about thawing out my hands so I could make deadline to enjoy the scene, but now it was coming back fast. So many pictures, so fast, all frozen in time, clicking through with the rapidity of a motor drive.

The good times and the bad. The frustrations and the joy.

I remember meeting him for the first time in 1977, when I was covering an Alabama game for the University of Tennessee student paper. I remember putting my tape recorder in front of him and being so disappointed later when I couldn't understand a word on it.

I remember how relieved he looked following the victory over Auburn when he won No. 315. I remember the pained, hurt look on his face, almost embarrassed, as he talked following the loss to Southern Miss, which ended the 57-game winning streak at Bryant-Denny Stadium.

I remember the last interview the morning of the Liberty Bowl, when I finally saw him as a lovable old man, instead of that giant on the cover of *Sports Illustrated*.

After the farewell interview, Bryant moved over to the couch for a group picture with the writers. After the picture, we all went over to shake hands with him, wishing him well. He looked at all of us, saying softly:

"I wonder what I'll be doing a year from today."

Then the funeral.

And the motorcade past Bryant-Denny, when the little kids rubbed their eyes and even the dogs looked sad.

And the ride into Elmwood, where a trail of tears followed the white hearse carrying his body.

Photographs and memories, that's all we have left of him now.

Somehow, it just doesn't seem right that the Alabama brochure has a young man pictured on the cover. It doesn't seem right that we won't have him to chuckle at on Sunday mornings. Nobody opened a bag of potato chips and a Coke better than he did.

That won't happen anymore.

What will Tuesday nights be without the Bear Line? We'll even miss the commercials.

"Have you called your mama today? I sure wish I could call mine."

And then there was the cute little girl coming to the door in the commercial and saying:

"Coach Bear, can Mary Harmon come out and play?"

No longer will there be that gruff voice at press conferences, that stubborn man, answering questions, but saying nothing.

Many sportswriters have some recollection of Bear Bryant. There were many who knew him well, those whom he confided in, whom he shared drinks with on gray nights in one-horse towns. Those he called friend.

Maybe I'll tell my grandchildren one day that we'd shared an occasional bottle of Jack Daniel's, that I bummed Chesterfields a time or two.

But I didn't.

I'll probably tell them that I was his friend.

But I wasn't.

Sure, I talked to him every Monday morning during the football season. And I asked him how he was doing, and how come Linnie Patrick didn't carry the ball more?

He answered me.

I think.

He even called me by my first name once or twice in three years.

He was polite. He never failed to return a call.

I tried to act like it was no big deal, talking to Bear Bryant. After all, young journalists aren't supposed to be impressed talking to famous people.

But I never failed to tell my coworkers that the Bear and I chewed the fat earlier in the day.

I also talked to Pat Dye on Monday mornings. But for some reason, nobody ever asked what he had to say.

Just Bear.

I called him Coach Bryant. I wanted to call him Bear or even Paul.

But none of that really matters anymore.

A new football season is on the horizon, a new era set to begin.

There is a new coach and a new offense. A new type of uniform and a new philosophy. There is a new radio announcer, a new host for the television show.

But there was only one Bear.

This was my first column at the Birmingham Post-Herald *and one of my all-time favorites. I have always found it interesting that my editors waited until after Bryant was gone to give me a column. Smart thinking by the editors. It would have been interesting to have written opinion pieces about Bryant during his tenure. Of course, had I done so, I might be at the bottom of a river instead of here today.*

SEPTEMBER 21, 1983

The sting of defeat still pains War Eagles

AUBURN—The clouds over this lovely village seem a little smaller this week, now that the Auburn football players' heads are no longer in them.

Maybe now reality will come back to this campus. Maybe now Auburn fans will quit believing *Playboy* and go back to the *Farmer's Almanac*.

Auburn flirted with the big time Saturday against Texas. It had about the same success as Custer at Little Big Horn.

But Coach Pat Dye did prove just how fortunate he is. The alumni purchased the mortgage on his $412,000 home before the Texas game. If they had waited until afterward, the only gift the alumni might have given him was a road map back to Wyoming.

Actually, things aren't that bad down here. Nobody is pushing the panic button. They're trying to forget Texas and concentrate on Tennessee.

And on the outside, most seem to be doing it. But whether or not this bunch can forget Texas remains to be seen.

Still, Dye seemed a little defensive yesterday at his weekly press conference when asked about two subjects: Auburn's national image in the wake of the loss and whether he is going to stick with quarterback Randy Campbell.

Neither the image nor Campbell came out of the Texas loss looking too good.

Dye said he is going with Campbell Saturday against Tennessee.

Campbell was not impressive in Saturday's game. In his defense, the line did little to help. But there were times when the senior quarterback showed he is simply not quick enough to get out of a jam.

As for his passing, well, it was pathetic. Campbell was 3 out of 13 for 25 yards and 1 interception. Against Southern Miss, he was 4 of 13 for 62 yards.

Overall his passing percentage for two games is 26.9, not exactly in Dan Fouts's league.

Dye said Pat Washington, Campbell's backup, is talented but not ready to handle the pressure.

Washington agreed with the head coach.

"As far as having the experience, I'm just not ready to play. I may not handle the pressure as well as Randy."

But if Campbell's play doesn't improve, Auburn will have problems this season.

Meanwhile, Dye said he refused to believe that one loss would hurt Auburn's national championship aspirations.

Of course, if Auburn comes through and wins the rest of its games, Dye's statement will hold up.

But the fact remains that Saturday's game was very important for bolstering Auburn's national image. Some in the press wrote last week that the Auburn-Texas game was one of the most important in recent history.

The fact that the Tigers were beaten so soundly right off the bat has to hurt their image. Of course, the Auburn folks, as well as some in the press, have talked and written about how the Tigers whipped Texas in the second half.

Big deal.

The bottom line was the final score, not how many first downs the Tigers got in the final two quarters.

Last year, Alabama dominated the stats against Auburn (507 to 257 in total yards) only to lose 23-22.

Dye said yesterday he never predicted a national title.

"I don't think I've ever been quoted as saying we would win a national championship. I think we have the type of caliber team that could, and I still do. The polls will take care of themselves."

"On a week-to-week basis, they don't mean anything. Tennessee is not even ranked, but they are probably better than half the teams that are. Maybe even better than us. Anybody who thought we'd go undefeated was an idiot."

Whether Dye predicted an undefeated season or not, he certainly did nothing to discourage national championship talk.

He didn't tell Auburn fans they were wrong to believe the preseason predictions.

So Auburn fans believed.

But Saturday, many found out that it takes more than hot air to be a national contender.

This was the first truly controversial column I wrote. The reaction to it was swift, with the phone lines lighting up at the newspaper. It caused such a commotion that I wrote a follow-up the next day, saying: "Frankly, it surprised me that some of you Auburn fans could take time out from milking cows and plowing the field to call. I hope this doesn't mean dairy prices are going up next year." Auburn crushed Tennessee the following weekend at Knoxville, and Pat Dye credited the two columns for being the difference in the game. Dye read the column to his team before the game, invalidating rumors he couldn't read.

DECEMBER 2, 1983

'70s champs turning into '80s chumps

TUSCALOOSA—It is easy to criticize Ray Perkins and say he has done a poor job of coaching this season's Alabama football team. You could maybe even say Alabama made a mistake in hiring him.

After all, his team has been an embarrassment of late, and the prospects are not great against Auburn or SMU.

On the other hand, Perkins didn't exactly inherit the greatest bunch of athletes in the school's history. This group lost two and tied one in 1981, dropped four in 1982 and have been losers three times in 1983.

Over the last 14 games, Alabama has an 8-6 record. And if the Tide drops the last two games—as the bookies predict—Alabama will be at .500 for the last 16 games.

Not exactly the record of a champion.

So whose fault is it that Alabama football has become mediocre? Why has the Crimson Tide become a bunch of second-class citizens behind their cross-state cousins in Auburn?

The answers are few and far between.

Nobody has come up with a clear explanation why the winningest football team in the nation in the '70s has become a bunch of also-rans in the '80s.

For some reason, the Alabama tradition just doesn't seem to be ingrained in this group of upperclassmen. Take the Crimson jerseys off, and you've got a run-of-the-mill football team.

There has been a lot of bad news at Alabama lately. The good news is this group of seniors will be gone in three weeks—which should be a fine Christmas present for Perkins and the frustrated Alabama faithful.

Although Perkins and his staff deny it, something seems to be wrong with the leadership on the team.

Maybe the team has lost so often that it doesn't seem to faze them anymore.

However, when you mention this to Perkins and his players, they shake their heads and say no.

"Our record over the last three years has not been what it has been (in the past)," Perkins said. "But to say that the players, coaches, or our true fans are just shrugging their shoulders after a loss—that is totally ridiculous.

"It hurts to lose."

Walter Lewis, the Tide's All-SEC quarterback, agreed.

"Losing is just like the devil," Lewis said. "Once you experience a little with the devil, you begin to feel a little guilty about what you did wrong. You can be lulled to sleep by the devil."

The devil aside, Alabama faces an interesting challenge tomorrow when it meets Auburn at Legion Field. It is always a big game. But rarely has Alabama been given so little chance of winning.

Auburn is ranked No. 3 in the nation and is headed to the Sugar Bowl. That's the kind of company Alabama used to keep.

And Auburn's success this season seems to be a sore spot with Perkins.

"To say it doesn't bother me would be lying," he said. "But at the same time, I respect what they've done. They didn't do it in a year. I have no questions that we'll come back. As far as the pendulum [swinging toward Auburn], it swung that way before and it has always swung back."

Another sore spot with Perkins is a rumor going around that he "begged for the Auburn job" when Doug Barfield was fired in 1980.

It is not clear if Auburn alumni began spreading the rumor, but it has gotten back to Perkins several times.

"That is ridiculous that I begged for the Auburn job," Perkins said. "That's as ridiculous as the story that Coach Bryant begged Pat Dye not to go to Auburn. I was called about the Auburn job and asked if I wanted to apply. I said no. I've never applied for a job, much less begged for an interview.

"Here I am with the New York Giants and can you imagine me begging for an interview at Auburn? Does that make sense?"

While Perkins took the Giants to a playoff berth in his third year, he has little to say about the team he left behind. The Giants have looked pitiful en route to a 3-9-1 record.

Asked how he would feel if things had been different and he'd been coaching the Giants this season, Perkins replied:

"I don't think about what would have been or what might have happened."

One might say the Giants would have been better off with Perkins than Bill Parcells. Perkins is certainly a more experienced head coach.

However, while Perkins did get the Giants in the playoffs in his third season, his overall record in New York was only 23-24. Of course, the first two years were mostly rebuilding.

When you count this season's mark, Perkins has an overall head coaching record of 30-37.

For Perkins, it has been both an interesting and a trying year. He admits it has been disappointing. But he also points out that it's not over yet.

There is still Auburn to play, as well as a Sun Bowl encounter in El Paso against SMU.

Perkins has made many changes since showing up in early January. He has made many people happy. He has made many mad.

So the question put to him seemed simple enough.

Do you have any regrets?

Perkins, sitting behind the desk that once belonged to college football's greatest and perhaps most humble coach, looked straight ahead with an ice-cold stare and replied:

"None."

This column came after an interview with Perkins, which was always a joy. Much the same as having four wisdom teeth yanked without Novocaine.

SEPTEMBER 5, 1984

Tide-Tiger relations heating up

It's only the the fifth day of September and already the nasty letters have started coming in. Apparently, Auburn fans are upset about some remarks made in this column last week about the loss to Miami.

That's the one thing I've never understood about football fans. Instead of getting upset with a sportswriter, who has nothing to do with the planning or outcome of the game, why don't they get mad at the head coach? He's the one who blew the Miami game, not me.

He's the one making the big bucks, the one being heralded as a genius all over the country.

Oh, Pat Dye did take the blame for the loss against Miami, saying he did a poor job of preparation.

No kidding!

If Pat had been a general at D-Day and used the same kind of preparation he did for Miami, this column would be written in German and the big football game of the year would be Schleswig and Dusseldorf instead of Alabama-Auburn.

Of course, we read now that Pat is down after the loss, that he hardly wants to talk about it anymore. I don't blame him. With the talent Dye has, and when you consider what a lousy job he did in getting them ready, I wouldn't have much to say either. About the only consolation Dye has is that he coaches Auburn and not Samford. After losing 82-9 last weekend, Samford would be wise to fold the team while it can still keep the opponents under 100 points.

Of course, if Pat is really depressed, he can always talk to Bo "It was just a practice game" Jackson.

While all of that is going on, the fans of Auburn are doing themselves proud by writing nasty missives filled with three-letter initials and four-letter words.

Perhaps the most interesting comments from Auburn fans are about how Boston College's Doug Flutie will tear up the Crimson Tide this weekend. It's like one game really has something to do with the other.

This all may serve to reveal that the Alabama-Auburn rivalry is hotter than ever.

I've had people call and say they have come close to fisticuffs with Alabama fans. I know the rivalry is intense, but this may be taking things a little too far.

But for some reason, this year is a little different.

For years I've heard from representatives of both camps about how they cheer for each other's school until the last regular game of the year when, of course, they play each other. Frankly, I never believed a word of it. Especially from the Auburn fans.

However, when Auburn knocked off Alabama two years ago, it all began to change. Then, when the War Eagles did it again, apparently it was more than Crimson Tide fans could handle.

They turned on Pat Dye.

Alabama fans used to have nice things to say about Pat. After all, he was a former coach at the school and remained very friendly with many of the coaches.

But now, the comments about Dye have changed dramatically.

Alabama fans now accuse Pat of trying to be just like Bear Bryant. They say he talks like him, walks like him, and coaches like him.

They claim that Dye is just a big phony.

But if Pat was so much like Bryant, why didn't Larry Spangler let Dye—instead of Gary Busey—play Bryant in the upcoming movie "The Bear." He certainly could have won an Oscar for "acting" like a coach against Miami.

But let's give Pat the benefit of the doubt. He's only lost one game, albeit a pretty big one.

There are 11 games left, and as the Rhodes scholar candidate Bo Jackson said recently:

"We open our season in three weeks against Texas."

I have always felt the line about Dye being a general at D-Day was among the most piercing I've ever written.

SEPTEMBER 14, 1984

Forney still loyal to Bear

His voice was synonymous with Alabama football. That slow, Southern drawl blended in with the crowd noise as smoothly as bourbon with branch water.

You could sit in your living room or on the front porch steps in the woods and listen to him call the action, and think you were there. Sure, he often gave the wrong information. Many times, he was difficult to understand. But that really didn't matter.

Because he was there for all the great games, the wonderful, magical moments when Namath and Stabler and scores of others wore Crimson. When Alabama football stood for something. When the Tide had streaks such as 27 wins in a row instead of an 11-9 record over the last 20 games like they do now.

You heard John Forney during all of those times.

Now, you hardly hear him at all.

That wasn't the way Forney wanted it. He would have preferred calling Alabama football until the end. But it didn't work out that way.

Coach Paul "Bear" Bryant died.

When Ray Perkins arrived, there would be many changes. One of the first was a new play-by-play announcer to call Alabama football. It would turn out to be the most controversial decision of Perkins's first year.

"I didn't just get off the turnip truck," Forney said. "I knew what was going on. But nothing was definite."

Finally, in early June 1983, Bert Bank, who has produced Alabama broadcasts for a quarter of a century, called his old friend and told him it was over. Bank did mention the possibility of Forney being the color man.

Forney didn't want the job.

But he hardly had time to even think about it. Five days later, he woke up and on the front sports page of the *Birmingham Post-Herald* was the headline: "Forney replaced as voice of Alabama football."

Forney was surprised. His friends were angry.

"It wasn't a good feeling at all. But it was something I knew was coming. I'm in my fifties, and by then, you've taken some pretty good shots. You kind of go with the flow."

Although Forney was hurt, he didn't call the newspapers and blast Perkins. As a matter of fact, he chose not to talk to the press at all. He even wrote the man who got rid of him.

"I have a feeling that the furor was more than he expected—or I did either. I was very gratified by the reaction. I was really amazed at the response from people I didn't even know."

Finally, the furor died down. Forney's replacement, Paul Kennedy, turned out to be a superb replacement.

But to this day, the school has never done a thing to honor Forney. When asked about this, Forney just shakes his head. It is a subject he prefers not to discuss.

Forney joined the broadcast team in 1952 as a color announcer. He got paid $25 a game. Twelve years later, he took over as the play-by-play announcer.

"I was on the broadcast team under (coaches) Drew, Whitworth, and Bryant. I had done some interviews under Coach Thomas, so I really would have liked to have had a year under Ray. But now, that's all over and done with. I'm kind of glad I bowed out at the same time as Coach Bryant." In Forney's last years, he was often difficult to understand. After all, he is an advertising executive by trade, not a radio announcer.

"I don't think I ever missed any names. What I missed were yard lines. I had confidence in who did what. I just wasn't sure where. A pass play that went to the 12 I might say the 17. I would say I was sensitive to criticism. But I was well aware of the criticisms and I accepted it."

Often, Bryant would get calls on his radio show asking him to replace Forney. But the Bear stood firm.

"For somebody to tell him to do something was not the way to get him to do something," says Forney. "He had known me and my family since I was a kid. I think he had a very deep sense of loyalty. I just knew him and loved him."

A broadcasting career that spanned 30 years is full of many memorable moments. Forney has had a few that stand out above the rest.

"The most exciting, one that took the most out of me—I thought I was going to have a heart attack—was the 11-10 victory over Tennessee in 1966. I ended up shaking like a leaf.

"Of course, there was the 315 game [against Auburn] and many more."

It is over now for John Forney. But the memories will never die.

This column appeared several months after John was let go by Perkins. John was reluctant to blast Perkins because of his loyalty to the school. It was ironic that three years later, John and I became radio partners and close friends.

September 17, 1984

Football fortunes falling

Welcome to the State of Alabama, Losersville, USA. A state where the fans obviously take the game of college football more seriously than the players.

By now, you've probably heard that both of our two major-college football teams are 0-2. They say it's the first time in history.

Because of it, many people are now saying the football season is officially over. I don't remember it ever starting.

Nevertheless, the sight of those 0-2 marks makes one remember the verbiage of Anson Mount, the *Playboy* picker, who wrote recently that Auburn and Alabama would meet Dec. 1 at Legion Field for the national championship.

More than likely, the only thing at stake in that game will the host spot in the Hall of Fame Bowl.

What has happened to Alabama and Auburn remains a mystery on this mid-September morning. In Auburn's schedule, more than likely, the Tigers would be 2-0 and still ranked No. 1 in the nation.

Alabama is another story.

The Alabama football fortunes fell to a new low Saturday at Grant Field.

Ray Perkins, the Alabama head coach, has talked many times about the pride and class, something his predecessor at Alabama taught him.

But this team has no pride or class.

This team is a bunch of losers.

It's possible this may be the bunch of chumps who end the Crimson Tide's fabled record of 25 consecutive bowl appearances.

Since arriving at Alabama, Ray Perkins has changed many things. He's installed a new offense. He's changed the uniforms and the helmets. He's changed the announcers and the sponsors.

Now, Perkins seems intent on even changing the winning tradition.

There are probably more than a few Alabama fans who hope Gary Busey, who will be in town Thursday night for the premiere of "The Bear," will stick around to roam the sidelines for the next game with Southwestern Louisiana.

It's unlikely Busey could call plays any worse than Perkins's staff did Saturday. Certainly, he'd be able to motivate the team better.

Of course, if you can't make the SW Louisiana game in person, you can fork out $100 bucks to watch it at home on Tide Vision. Tide Vision could turn out to be to cable television what the Edsel was to the automobile industry.

Can you imagine anybody wasting $50, let alone 10 cents, to watch this football team play on television or in person?

We've all heard now that Alabama's record is 1-4 in the last five games and 9-9 in the last 18. This does not make Alabama fans a happy group. It's tough to swallow the fact that your school's football program, once the proudest in the nation, has become nothing but mediocre.

It's tough to accept that your team is no better than Georgia Tech and scores of other programs, whose primary goal is a winning record at the end of the season.

That's what Alabama fans face this morning.

At the other end of the state, Auburn fans are growling, too. But the bark doesn't seem to have the bite as it does with those who wear Crimson.

Auburn is 0-2. But Saturday night in Austin, at least they showed the desire to win. Their road may be rocky without Bo Jackson. Unlike Alabama, they're still on the road instead of in some ditch.

For Alabama, there are few bright spots. The injury to Vince Sutton, the freshman quarterback, could be a tough blow if he doesn't heal quickly. Mike Shula, the starting quarterback, has a nice ring to his name. But it's doubtful that even his own father would start him.

The offensive line is an utter joke. And the defense, that once proud unit, is a disgrace.

But what isn't at Alabama these days.

For Ray Perkins, the days ahead do not look promising. He knows that better than anyone.

People that care about Alabama football know something must be done soon to salvage this football program. Otherwise, Alabama fans had better start getting used to more Saturday afternoons like the last one.

The beginning of this column was picked up nationally by the Associated Press and ran in newspapers across the country. It did not make me many friends in the State of Alabama.

September 21, 1984

"The Bear" bombs out where the legend left his footprints

Bear Bryant spent most of his lifetime preaching pride and class to his players. It was part of the legend that made him the winningest coach in college football history.

But the movie about his life, which premiered here last night, had no class and was obviously produced with no pride.

What producer Larry Spangler originally had in mind was unclear. But one thing is clear. This movie was not worth all the controversy. It was a total waste of time. And unless you have money to burn, stay home and wait for it to hit television. It won't be long.

This is the kind of schlock that belongs in drive-in theaters or on Showtime after hours.

What could have been a tremendous story is honest depiction of a great man's life, as a disaster.

But we should have known better three years ago, when it was announced that Spangler was producing it. After all, this man's greatest claim to fame was producing *The Legend of Nigger Charley* and its sequel *The Soul of Nigger Charley*.

Of course, as for biographies, Spangler has ventured out twice, producing the forgettable biography of American artist Andrew Wyeth and the equally forgettable story of French designer Coco Chanel.

Hopefully, "The Bear" will be Spangler's last biography as well as his last picture.

Despite the poor manner in which it was put together, it did have some interesting moments. It takes the viewer through the career of Bryant. It shows him wrestling a large bear to get his nickname. It takes him through coaching jobs at Maryland and Texas A&M on through the glory days at Alabama, ending with his final game at the Liberty Bowl.

There are some touching moments, particularly when Bryant is shown courting Mary Harmon. The scenes at Texas A&M also were interesting. But the movie jumped around so much, it was difficult to keep from getting seasick.

Few story lines were developed. The viewer yearned for more. Wouldn't it have been interesting to deal with the NCAA censure of Bryant for cheating at Texas A&M? The scenes showing Bryant at Grand Junction, when he worked the players day and night was one of the few highlights.

The movie spent little time with *The Saturday Evening Post* suit. It was never explained how much torment Bryant suffered through this period.

One of the most interesting moments dealt with Bryant's return to Alabama. The film showed four alumni sitting around talking about how the program had fallen apart. It was apparent the scene rang a current ring to some in the audience.

One of the lightest moments in the movie showed Bryant and Mary Harmon shopping for a new hat after they arrived in Tuscaloosa.

When Bryant tried on an ugly hat, Mary Harmon said:

"Oh, my God."

Bryant smiled, then said, "You can call me Paul in public."

There were several other laughs in the movie. But the biggest laugh was the movie itself.

Although Spangler claimed to have done years of research, there were moments in the movie that were simply not factual.

The 1981 Alabama-Auburn game, where Bryant won No. 315, ended in the cold darkness of Legion Field. But in the movie, Bryant is shown being carried off the field with the sun shining down on him.

As for the acting, Gary Busey did a commendable job playing Bryant. Interestingly, Busey, who is 39, did a far superior job portraying Bryant at 60 than he did the younger Bear.

But the biggest fault, although one can't blame the actor, was the noticeable absence of Bryant's salty language, almost as much his trademark as his houndstooth hat.

In the movie, Bryant used words such as "shoot" when dressing down a player. But not often.

While the movie was being shown. Busey paced back and forth in the lobby. He kept going in and out of the theater.

This reporter followed him out at one interval. The actor was asked if he felt the absence of Bryant's salty language made it difficult for the movie to be an honest portrayal.

Busey grunted. "Who gives a --— about that. I was just reading from the damn script."

With that kind of attitude from the star, it was no wonder "The Bear" was a bomb.

This was the first and last movie review I did for the Post-Herald. *An official with Cobb Theaters seriously tried to have me banned from his cinemas after the column.*

DECEMBER 3, 1984

"Temporary insanity" is Dye's best defense

Pat Dye has done wonders for Auburn University since taking over for Doug Barfield four years ago. He inherited a program in shambles and brought unity and spirit back to the campus. He also recruited top-notch football players and led the Tigers to an SEC championship one year ago.

But Saturday afternoon, in a moment that may go down in athletic infamy, the Auburn coach may have lost so much he has worked to build.

In perhaps the most inexplicable decision football fans here have ever witnessed, Pat Dye threw away a victory against Auburn's biggest rival, a million dollar trip to the Sugar Bowl, and perhaps, the unyielding confidence so many have entrusted to him since signing on four years ago.

Instead of kicking the field goal for the win, the Tigers were saddled with a stunning 17-15 loss that left many of the 76,853 fans at Legion Field shaking their heads.

According to the records, Dye is a graduate of the University of Georgia. He was such a good student that he made Academic All-American in 1960. So the man is not stupid.

Therefore, the only explanation of Dye's decision to go for a touchdown on fourth-and-one from the one-foot line instead of kicking a chip-shot field goal is that he lost his senses. If it were a court of law, there is little doubt the bench would allow Dye to enter a plea of temporary insanity.

But in the aftermath, Dye refused to back down. He said he made the right decision. That comment is tantamount to George Custer saying he made the right decision at the Little Big Horn.

Of course, Dye was quick to place the blame on the very sore shoulders of Bo Jackson.

"If I had known Bo was going the wrong way, I would have called for the field goal," said Dye.

Perhaps, since Auburn had already played 11 games this season, Jackson figured the Iron Bowl was another practice game. After all, isn't that what he said about the season opener against Miami?

Actually, the play Dye called was a 56 combo—a sweep to the right. Jackson thought the play was a 57 combo, which goes the other way.

While Bo spends another off-season working on his Heisman Trophy acceptance speech, maybe he can take a moment or two to also learn the playbook.

Regardless, when the experts remember back to the college football season of 1984, Dye's gamble will go down as perhaps the most single, imbecilic call of the year.

For the Liberty Bowl game against Arkansas, Dye ought to throw away his Auburn baseball cap and wear a dunce hat instead.

Almost everyone around here remembers that Bear Bryant coached his last game in the Liberty Bowl a few years back. For a few moments Saturday afternoon, there were probably a few Auburn fans who were hoping Dye would do the same thing.

Going to the Liberty Bowl instead of the Sugar will take some getting used to for Auburn fans.

All week long, Dye used the warm 72-degree temperature of the Louisiana Superdome as a motivational reminder against the bitter cold of Memphis on a December night. Last year, the Liberty Bowl was played in 17-degree weather. The year before, in Bear Bryant's finale, it was below freezing.

"Coach Dye told us all week it was up to us," said Pat Washington, the Auburn quarterback.

"He said the Superdome was warm while it could get pretty cold in Memphis."

Of course, the Liberty Bowl is better than no bowl at all, something Alabama will face for the first time in 25 years. The victory over its bitter rival will give Alabama something solid on which to build for the future.

While the season was a nightmare for Alabama followers,

Coach Ray Perkins and his staff were able to hold the team together through some very trying times. The future looks much brighter today than it did two months ago. But no matter how you cut it, it was a dreary year.

Much like the off-season will be for Pat Dye and his staff.

Whether the game turns out to be an athletic benchmark of sorts or not, remains to be seen. But we learned one thing: No matter now hard a team tries to win, the outcome can be decided by a coach.

So it is wrong to blame the Auburn players for Saturday's 17-15 loss. If anyone is to blame, it is clearly Pat Dye.

For it was his stupidity, and his alone, that decided the outcome of this contest.

One of the toughest columns I ever did on Dye. Some people felt the criticism about his mental state was unfair. I felt like by giving Dye the "diminished capacity defense," I was being kind.

FEBRUARY 18, 1985

Some fans are still bigoted

In the days that have followed Sonny Smith's resignation at Auburn, many different reasons for the decision have been given. Perhaps the one that has drawn the most conversation is the issue of race.

In this space last week, there was discussion that pressure by State Finance Director Henry B. Steagall II, who is also the vice-chairman of the Board of Trustees, may have played a part in Smith's frustration at Auburn, which eventually led to his puzzling resignation.

Steagall "categorically denied" the report. Smith said that was not the reason he left, adding that Gov. George Wallace's top advisor never told him to recruit more white players.

But Steagall later admitted in an interview published in *The Atlanta Constitution* that he didn't recall the conversation, but....

"If I did say anything like that, it was in the context of trying to be helpful. It wasn't anything racial."

Certainly not. After all, why would anybody in Wallace's inner circle be thinking along those lines?

Nevertheless, a person connected to the Auburn program said that not only has Steagall mentioned the black-white issue to Smith, but according to the source, "so have a lot of other alumni."

In a sense, it is a tragedy when alumni base their support of a program on the color of an athlete's skin. But it happens.

It has long been my theory that one reason basketball has lagged far behind football in this state is the influx of the black athlete. I asked a colleague once why it didn't bother people as much in football, where there is also an abundance of black athletes.

"In football, you can't really see who is playing," said the person. "But in basketball, all they have on is shorts. It's not hard to tell what color they are."

However, both Auburn and Alabama have had their problems with black football players, too.

Charles Thomas, who started for Auburn in 1980, accused fans of being racists after a game in which he was soundly booed. Racial slurs were often used by Alabama fans when Walter Lewis had difficulty on the field.

I'll never forget walking the final holes with Lee Trevino and Gary Player at the PGA this summer. And when the scoreboard showed that Calvin Peete, a black man, was closing in on the leaders, some club members were horrified.

The actual comments from several members of Shoal Creek are not worthy of printing in a family newspaper.

Perhaps it's also a reason that auto racing is so popular in these parts. A well-known sportswriter in this state once told me he enjoyed auto racing because there are no blacks involved. Actually, his description was a little stronger than the aforementioned.

Whatever the genesis of all this, there is no disputing that black athletes are here to stay.

In the Southeastern Conference, there were a total of 154 players listed on the preseason rosters. The number of black players numbered 108, which translates to 70 percent.

As of last weekend, 40 of the 50 starters in the SEC are black. Only Vanderbilt has more whites starting than blacks—a total of four.

Alabama has two whites starting. Five teams—including Auburn—don't start a single white player.

UAB has three white players out of 13. None of them starts.

Of the nation's top three schools, only St. John's, the top team in the last poll, has a white starter. The Redmen have two while Georgetown and Memphis State have none.

However, the fact that Memphis State and Georgetown start all blacks has not kept the crowds down. It's hard to buy a ticket to watch the Hoyas play. In Memphis, it's nearly impossible.

But that is not the case in our state. While Saturday's night game between Alabama and Auburn was a sellout, tickets to most games go begging.

Part of the reason is the lack of interest here in basketball. Part of that reason is the predominance of black athletes.

Our society has come a long way since Dr. King led the famous march from Selma to Montgomery two decades ago. However, from the looks of things, the journey is far from over.

I always found it interesting to read the passage in this column about Shoal Creek that appeared five years before the controversy over a black member erupted into an international story.

MARCH 25, 1985

Villanova remembers its friend

As the clock ticked down and the Villanova players began celebrating their extraordinary 56-44 victory over North Carolina in the NCAA Southeast Regional final, the old man sat alone, motionless in his wheelchair. There was bedlam on every corner of the court, but he didn't move, except to occasionally tilt his back from one side to another.

To his left, he saw Rollie Massimino, his dear friend, being interviewed about the biggest victory of his career by Brent Musburger and Billy Packer on CBS. To his right, he saw the players, his players, hugging and kissing everyone in sight, before finally cutting down the nets.

Although he sat there showing little emotion, one got the feeling he would have done anything to be able to leap out of that chair and grab every player in sight. He was that proud.

But when you're 75 years old, and suffering from Lou Gehrig's disease, some things just aren't possible.

Finally, the Villanova players moved over to him. After slapping him on the back and high-fiving him (which must have been quite a treat for a man his age), they put the freshly-cut net around his neck.

To a bystander, it was difficult to avoid shedding a tear.

John "Jake" Nevin has seen it all in his lifetime. As trainer of Villanova for the last 56 years, there have been many celebrations. But few could top yesterday's victory. Perhaps that's why it was so meaningful to this elderly man.

A few minutes later, the celebration had moved from center court to the locker room. On a blackboard, someone had written, "Final Four in Lexington."

Nevin will be in Lexington, just like he has been everywhere else Villanova has played in the last half-century.

So there were plenty of reasons for him to celebrate.

As the players continued the hugging, Nevin pulled out a cigar, and lit up. When a reporter came up to him and asked if he had a moment to talk, Nevin motioned him over.

"This is wonderful," he said with a vintage Philadelphia accent. "It's such a great feeling. It's great for Rollie, and it's great for the program."

Whether he'll admit it or not, it's also great for Jake Nevin.

Since the beginning of time, or more precisely since 1929, Nevin has been a fixture around the Villanova sidelines. Last summer, his fight with Lou Gehrig's disease—a rare degenerative fatal disease affecting the spinal cord—began to slow him down.

He could no longer get around without a wheelchair. But the disease couldn't keep him away from the boys.

"The kids still feel real close to me," he said proudly. "This is great for them, and for Rollie. He's so good to the kids."

When somebody walked by to tug on the net around his neck, he nodded his appreciation.

"When they gave me the net, I told them to give it to somebody else. I've been there before."

Rollie Massimino has not.

Three times in the last seven years—in 1978, 1982, and 1983—Villanova has made it to the regional final, only to fall short. But yesterday, the Wildcats would not let the head coach down. And although they looked dreadful in the first half, causing Musburger to say off camera, "That's the worst half of basketball I've ever seen in my life," they came storming back in the final 20 minutes.

"He's just been so close," said Nevin. "It was so important for him to get to the Final Four."

A few feet from Nevin, Rollie Massimino Jr., the coach's boy, was also smiling. He was proud for his old man, but he was also happy for Nevin.

"He's just so much a part of Villanova," said young Massimino. "My dad is so close to him. He's like a father to him. Jake is always around the house, eating dinner with us."

Before the first game of the year, Massimino's dad, knowing that Jake Nevin was not well, dedicated the season to the longtime trainer.

"He's 75, and we knew we had to do it for him," said Massimino. "We knew he wasn't doing well."

Massimino said that's why the players ran over to Nevin after the game to present him the net.

"At the end of the game, he couldn't get up and run over to us, so we ran over to him."

The end of the game was something special. But as the crowd at the Civic Center and a national television audience watched, Nevin looked away. At several points, his eyes appeared shut.

"People think I was sleeping at the end of the game, but I'm not sleeping," said Nevin. "I was saying prayers."

"And oh yes," he said: "They were answered."

A personal favorite, because of the emotion of the event. It was just a wonderful sight to see Nevin celebrating. Two weeks later, he had a lot more to celebrate, as Villanova won the national title. He died a few months later.

SEPTEMBER 18, 1985

Auburn is No. 2, slipping

Do you ever wonder why Auburn fans have a chip on their shoulders? Well, consider this for just a moment.

Last Saturday, for the first time in the school's history, the Tigers entered Jordan-Hare Stadium as the nation's No. 1 team.

While Auburn wasn't playing Florida or Georgia, the opposition was decent.

In other words, Southern Mississippi is not in the cream puff division like Southwestern Louisiana and Cincinnati.

Now, the win over the Golden Eagles wasn't pretty, but the scene must have turned even uglier Sunday morning when Auburn fans picked up *The Birmingham News.*

At the top of the sports page was a story on the Alabama-Texas A&M game. The game was important, but with Alabama ranked No. 20 and the Aggies nowhere in the polls, it wasn't exactly a battle for the MacArthur Bowl.

There were actually two stories about Alabama, and at the bottom, a story about the game between the nation's top-ranked team and Southern Miss.

This is not meant as a criticism of the *News*. Frankly, I think they made the right decision in playing Alabama over Auburn.

I had a choice of attending the two games myself. I chose the Alabama game. Why? Because it was played in Birmingham, where I work and live. And people in my business—and others—will continue to have that attitude as long as Auburn's athletic department turns its back on the city.

Don't be surprised if Auburn slips from No. 2 in town to No. 3 next year if, somehow, the Stallions survive and the USFL becomes a viable league.

Auburn has not made many friends in this community by taking its games out of Legion Field. There is little doubt the school's image will slip further if Pat Dye carries out his move to take the Alabama-Auburn game to Jordan-Hare Stadium.

That's Auburn's choice. But tell their fans not to bother to call and complain to the newspaper about where their stories appear.

After all, it was Ray Perkins who recently pledged to play at least three games in Birmingham for as long as he is coach.

Pat Dye is rather silent when the question of Birmingham comes up.

All Dye talks about is moving the Alabama-Auburn game out of town. By playing in Birmingham, the Crimson Tide is giving the hotel and restaurant industry a boost.

Of course, the Auburn home games really make an impact on that city's wonderful restaurants and hotels.

From here, it seems the only people who benefit are the Kentucky Fried Chicken and the Dairy Queen on 280 near Dadeville.

Maybe even the Stuckey's on I-65 does well, too.

What's even more amazing is that Auburn folks keep talking about expanding Jordan-Hare Stadium. At the same time, they can't even fill it up for all of their games. There have been close to 25,000 empty seats for the first two games.

True, the students have not come back to school. But that might be a reason for moving one of the early games to Legion Field.

Certainly, the Auburn-Southern Miss game would have sold out Legion Field.

In a sense, it's ridiculous to argue over who gets how much space in a newspaper. Both schools probably get more than they should.

But believe it or not, people actually keep a running count of which team gets more ink.

On the other hand, it shouldn't surprise Auburn fans when they get second billing if their team is playing at Jordan-Hare while Alabama is at Legion Field.

It's really too bad this subject must even be discussed. With Auburn at the top of the rankings, this should be a glorious time for the school.

Yet, facts are facts.

Auburn may be the No. 1 team in the nation. But in Birmingham, because of their ways, they are clearly No. 2 ... and slipping.

With the possibility of UAB football, the headline might need to be amended to: Auburn is No. 3, slipping.

December 30, 1985

Welcome to state No. 50

HONOLULU—After telling the cab driver the destination, the usual banter began. Whether you're in Manhattan or Maui, some things never change.

At least, that's what I thought.

"Your first trip to Hawaii," said the man whose identification described him as Daniel Kim.

"You got it," I said. "I'm here for the Aloha Bowl."

"Yes," said Kim, with a smile. "That's nice."

"Well, who do you like?"

"Oh, I don't know," said Kim, somewhat puzzled. After a moment of silence, he replied, "Who's playing?"

After explaining that Alabama and USC were in town, he smiled, and said: "I like baseball."

"The Dodgers and the Giants," I said, figuring they were the closest teams.

"No," he said. "My team is in Korea."

I was afraid to ask whether it was in North or South Korea.

Anyway, welcome to Hawaii. And while it may be the 50th state, I don't think there is any threat of football ever overtaking surfing and sunbathing as the national pastimes out here.

People here have about as much interest in football as we on the mainland have in the USFL. Anybody who wondered about interest only had to count the crowd Saturday night at the Aloha Bowl.

Still, this is a beautiful place to visit. It seems like the tourists here have plenty of money. Or did.

There are McDonald's on every corner of Waikiki—letting visitors know that even over here, you can get two all-beef patties, special sauce, lettuce, cheese, pickles, and onions on a sesame bun for under two bucks.

Of course, sushi is big around here, too. As is, or so it seems, half of Japan.

In Alabama, many of us go to Gulf Shores or Destin for the weekend. In Tokyo, they drive their Chevy trucks to the airport, and head to Hawaii.

The popular saying around here about the Japanese is: "First, they bombed us, now they bought us."

It's expensive here, too.

My first night here, I was too exhausted to even stand. So I thought I'd do a very American kind of thing, and order room service.

I ordered a fruit salad and an iced tea.

The tea cost $3.25. The fruit salad only set me back $10.25.

Of course, a room at the Sheraton Waikiki, where Alabama stayed, costs $139 for a single. That's the cheapest room. For $539 you can get a suite. I hope Ray Perkins enjoyed his.

About the only cheap place to sleep is the beach.

The time difference also takes a lot of getting used to. My first morning here, I was out of bed by 2 a.m. (6 a.m. Birmingham time). It got a little better as the week went on, but not much.

Television is the real killer.

The San Francisco-New York NFL playoff game began yesterday at 8 a.m.

"That's the way to watch football," said Perkins."You wake up, grab a cup of coffee, and see the game. Then, you go play golf."

The Sun Bowl game between Georgia and Arizona began Saturday morning at 7:30 a.m.

The television news is also something. The sports is funny, too. On the 6 p.m. newscast, they already are giving the college basketball results.

As I mentioned earlier, there is plenty of American food. But they have their own specialty foods out here. On almost every corner, there is a Macadamia Nut store. Jim Nabors has a nut farm in Maui.

Of course, they push Dole pineapples fairly heavily out here, too.

Naturally, the big tourist attraction for most of the Alabama visitors was Pearl Harbor. It is an eerie sight looking at the historic Arizona Memorial, where so many servicemen perished. But I found something a little disturbing about the hucksterism involved with it.

Others here did, too.

One of the members of the Alabama official party, who will remain nameless, commented:

"It's really ridiculous for Americans to have a monument for one of the biggest blunders in our history. Doing this is tantamount to Pat Dye constructing a monument on the 1-yard line at Legion Field honoring the spot where Bo went the wrong way."

When I heard that comment, I immediately looked around for Steve McGarrett of Hawaii 5-0 fame. He wasn't around, but if he had been, I feel certain he would have turned to his left, and ordered:

"Book 'em, Danno. Murder one."

I never cared for Ray Perkins while he was coaching at Alabama. However, by having a mediocre year, Alabama went to the Aloha Bowl and I got a free trip to Honolulu. Of course, it did get a bit scary when Jerry Duncan, Doug Layton, and myself yelled "Tora, Tora, Tora," to a Japanese couple on the beach. I learned how to run very quickly on the beach.

MARCH 28, 1986

Brown can thrill, chill a reporter

Perhaps the easiest assignment in sports journalism is being sent to interview Dale Brown, the fiery basketball coach at LSU. You ask him a simple yes or no question and when he finishes answering 90 minutes later, you say thank you and go home.

Of course, in this business, getting a coach to answer your questions clearly is not always easy. Anyone who has ever tried getting a straight answer from Pat Dye can attest to that.

But when the LSU basketball coach shows up in Dallas today at a news conference preceding the Final Four, it's likely the horde of reporters will lap it up like a kitten with warm milk.

Since getting into this business seven years ago, I have met and covered a number of coaches. But rarely have I gotten to know—and respect—one quite like I did Brown.

He played a small part in helping me get my first newspaper job in Louisiana. I still haven't forgiven him for that.

Today, as Brown prepares his team for his second Final Four in five years, he is the envy of hundreds of college basketball coaches.

Although many would like to be in his shoes this morning, it's unlikely they would have traded places with Brown some 50 years ago.

It began for Brown in Minot, North Dakota. Three days after he was born, his father picked up and left town. Brown wouldn't see him again for 20 years.

Brown and his mother lived on a $42.50-a-month welfare check in a one-room walkup above a noisy neighborhood bar. Brown was a brash little kid, always getting into scrapes.

When he came home with his nose bloodied and his eyes shut one night, his mother pleaded with him to stop fighting and help her survive.

It was then that Brown discovered basketball.

"Basketball gave me discipline, goals, and guidance. It was a catalyst to save my life. It was a father substitute."

Now, he is a father to his players. And every other stray dog that comes along.

Last week, I was chatting with Brown in the hours leading up to LSU's regional semifinal with Georgia Tech at the Omni in Atlanta. As we were talking, Brown spotted a blind man a few feet away. Immediately, Brown introduced himself and began talking about the man's courage to fight a handicap.

Brown has made many friends this way. But he's also made a basket full of enemies along the highway.

Several years ago, he was invited to speak to a group in Huntsville.

"Prior to my speech, a prominent member of the community was telling a story to the group that slandered blacks," Brown said.

A few minutes later, Brown excused himself and went into the kitchen and apologized to the help.

They told him slander against their race was a way of life.

Brown, a card-carrying member of the NAACP, occasionally carries things too far.

Once, Brown took his 15-year old daughter to Gainesville for a game against Florida. She sat on the bench during the game, which infuriated a few unruly fans.

"So what do I hear from the stands. 'Hey Brown, you bring yourself a little whore on the trip now.'

"One sports editor criticized me saying, 'If Brown learned anything on the trip, it's that a 15-year-old doesn't belong on the bench during a college basketball game.' That's sick. He's lost the total message."

Brown has been stung by press criticism.

"John Wooden was despised when he won; Adolph Rupp was too. Bobby Knight is. You tell me a winner who is not."

Still, one of the most vivid memories of Brown occurred in Baton Rouge several years ago following a tough win.

The press had gathered in his office and was going through the usual give-and-take that occurs after a game. A reporter asked Brown why he switched LSU from man-to-man defense to a zone late in the game. Instead of answering, Brown waved the startled reporter to the chalkboard in his office and said:

"Why don't you diagram the difference between the two defenses on the board for everybody? Go ahead, show everybody how you run a 2-3 zone."

The reporter turned as white as a ghost. He couldn't have drawn the play for all the money in Imelda Marcos's Swiss bank account.

But as usual, Dale Brown had made his point.

As you could tell from this column, Dale Brown has always been one of my favorite subjects. If I were a basketball coach, something tells me I would be like Dale.

MAY 5, 1986

Another old pro proves that age can be beaten

TALLADEGA— It had been 55 races since Robert Arthur Allison pulled his car into victory lane, an insufferable drought for a driver of his magnitude. But on the eve of the Winston 500, one of the biggest events on the NASCAR circuit, one got the impression that Allison was on the verge of another victory.

"I've never been happier in my life," said the 48-year old grandfather from Hueytown. "Things are coming together for us. Time is the only thing standing between our effort and victory lane."

And yesterday, in front of a record crowd estimated at 130,000 fans, Bobby Allison's prophecy proved correct. He turned back the field—as well as the hard-charging Dale Earnhardt—to capture first prize in the storied event.

Naturally, one of the first subjects brought up here yesterday was the comparison between Allison's victory and those of Jack Nicklaus in the Masters and Willie Shoemaker in the Kentucky Derby.

"It feels good," Allison said about the comparison. "And you tell those youngsters to hang in there.

Although comparing the victory to the other two makes great copy, in reality, the circumstances between Allison and Nicklaus are far different.

First of all, the sports are not comparable. No matter how great a race driver is, without a good car and crew he has no more chance of winning then Leon Spinks—the worst driver since the invention of the wheel.

And while Allison has rarely been in victory lane the past two years, this season has been a different story.

Since leaving the old DiGard team for the Stavola Brothers, Allison has come close to winning several times. This year, Allison has had six top-ten finishes. And remember, it's only been three years since Allison won the Grand National points championship—the highlight of his spectacular career.

Still, the experts these days don't judge you on fourth-place finishes. No one cares if you come in third in the Valleydale Meats 500 or fourth in the First Union Bank 400.

It's the majors that matters.

Victories in the majors have been few and far between lately for Allison.

His last major victory was at the World 600 at Charlotte, North Carolina, in 1984. The last victory at Daytona was in 1982, when he won both major races. He last won at Talladega in 1981.

Still, there were plenty of anxious moments for the famed leader of the Alabama Gang. As he trailed Bill Elliot with 14 laps to go in the 188-lap marathon, there weren't many in the crowd who felt he could beat the greatest driver in the sport today.

Lucky for Allison, however, Elliot blew his engine and saw the end of the race from the garage.

But the question remained: Could Allison have beaten Elliot?

"Not unless he let me," Allison said in a remarkable display of candor.

Whenever a Nicklaus or Shoemaker or now an Allison wins a major sporting event, the inevitable question is, will the person retire?

"I really haven't thought much about retirement," he said. "I've hung in there when times were tough and come back from that. Last year was a trying time for me. It made me realize just how competitive our sport has become and how important total organization is in running a race team."

After three volatile years with the DiGard race team, Allison left and joined the Stavola team for this season. It has worked like a charm.

"They have been great to work with. This win is especially sweet because of what happened last year (with DiGard).

Allison, the oldest driver to win this event, was asked how special it was to win at his age.

"You'll never understand the feeling until you're 48 years old and try to get out of bed in the morning."

The victory was also sweet because it occurred at Allison's home track.

"I can't think of a better place to win than to have 75,000 screaming Alabamians."

Actually, there were about 130,000 fans, according to Jim Freeman, the director of public relations at the speedway. Obviously, not all of them were from Alabama.

Freeman said about 30 percent of the fans in the grandstand and 70 percent in the infield are Alabamians.

While the speedway officials were thrilled with the record crowd, even they admitted some people show up just to drink beer, watch women, and see a crash.

"People don't want to see anybody hurt," Freeman said. "But if there's going to be a crash, they want to see it."

Those who came here yesterday to watch a spectacular crash had to leave disappointed.

But it's unlikely that many left with long faces. After all, Bobby Allison had turned the clock back once again with his extraordinary victory.

One couldn't help but feel happy for him.

I have never professed to be a big racing fan, however Allison's victory was stirring and emotional. It would be his last at Talladega.

JANUARY 1, 1987

Perkins may be another bad deal for Bucs

When the great ringmaster P. T. Barnum remarked that there's a sucker born every minute, he wasn't talking about football.

But he didn't know Hugh Culverhouse.

Culverhouse, who owns the worst team in professional football—the Tampa Bay Buccaneers—has never shown much savvy when it comes to hiring coaches.

He stayed with John McKay long past his prime. And Culverhouse was the only owner in the NFL who would have anything to do with Leman Bennett, who won four games in two years before he was fired.

And who can forget Culverhouse's bungling of the Bo Jackson affair?

Culverhouse's decision yesterday to "buy" Perkins from the University of Alabama proves some things never change.

Culverhouse reportedly is paying Perkins $750,000 per year. He might even give him a piece of the franchise.

All of this could turn out to be the worst business since New Coke.

In four years with the New York Giants, Perkins had a 24-35 record. At Alabama, things got a little better, but coaching the school through its first losing season in 25 years, plus a couple of Sun Bowls and an Aloha Bowl, hardly qualifies Perkins for the College Football Hall of Fame.

There are at least a dozen NFL coaches better qualified or more deserving of the kind of money Perkins is receiving. Even Perkins admitted he probably isn't worth it.

Perhaps Culverhouse was trying to make a large contribution to Alabama by taking Perkins off the Crimson Tide's hands in time to beat the tax law changes.

Perkins won a couple of big football games at Alabama. But he isn't Don Shula or Bill Walsh. Or even Mike Ditka, who makes far less as coach of the Chicago Bears.

What's even more amazing was to listen to some of the remarks Culverhouse made after meeting Perkins for the first time.

"I can say one of the pleasant mornings I've ever spent was talking with Ray Perkins," said Culverhouse. "I spent a sleepless night Sunday, prior to our press conference here (to announce Bennett was fired). When I went up to see him (at the Hyatt) and it was 10 o'clock. He said, 'Do you feel like talking?' I thought maybe 10 minutes because I was ready to hit the sack. For the next seven hours I didn't even know there was any time passing by. It was an exciting conversation and dialogue. I guess in the movies they call it body chemistry."

It really makes you wonder if it was really Perkins he was talking to. Either that, or Perkins got a personality transplant while he was in El Paso, Texas, last week.

Maybe Perkins will get along better with the fans and media in Tampa than he has at either of his stops in New York or Tuscaloosa. But it is doubtful.

At the press conference yesterday, Perkins was asked if it bothered him so few people cared he was leaving.

"I apologize to the people who think I ruffled some feathers when I came in," he said. "I wasn't here for a personality contest."

Perkins also was asked whether departing, just months after his $200,000 mortgage was paid off by Alabama boosters, bothered him.

"No," he said in typical Perkins fashion.

Do you have any intention of paying them back?

"If they want, I'll pay it back," he said.

Of course $200,000 is mere petty cash to Perkins now.

Perkins never won a national championship at Alabama. He didn't even take an SEC title. But he was quick to respond when asked if he considered his four years at Alabama a success.

"Hell, yes."

In some ways, it was.

Perkins kept Alabama out of trouble with the NCAA. He made giant strides in upgrading the athletic facilities. And Perkins obviously cared a great deal about academics.

But he didn't seem to care very much about people. And that's why many people in Alabama this morning are glad he's gone.

> *In many respects, I wrote this column with a great degree of sadness. I felt like Herb Block, the vinegary cartoonist of the* Washington Post, *when Nixon resigned. I didn't think it would ever be as good without Perkins. I was happily mistaken.*

JANUARY 5, 1987

Bravo for bold pick by Thomas

TUSCALOOSA—After being introduced as the new head football coach at the University of Alabama, Bill Curry wasted little time in thanking his wife, Carolyn.

"My wife and I have had 12 wonderful years of marriage," Curry said. "And we feel 12 of 24 is pretty good."

Incredibly, in only four seconds, Curry has displayed more personality than Ray Perkins had in four years.

Many followers of Alabama football are still seeing red this morning following the decision by Dr. Joab Thomas to go "outside the family" to hire the school's 21st football coach.

While the decision was puzzling at first, it is the view here that Thomas has made both a daring and historic choice.

Thomas said he got phone calls from "so-called" Alabama fans who threatened to withdraw their support unless one of eight or so leading contenders was picked. Some even wanted him fired.

"I had to take the phone off the hook," Thomas said. "Some of them were nasty.

"A growing constituency of concerned people will applaud this kind of appointment. Two years from now when we win the national championship, there will be a lot more people applauding this kind of appointment."

For the first time in this part of the country, a college president has put academics on no less than an even keel with winning.

Secondly, Thomas has told the sports world in a subliminal way that he is fed up with coaches such as Ray Perkins and Jackie Sherrill, who seem to enjoy ticking off people almost as much as winning national titles.

"There were several key things we looked at in our interviews," said a member of the search committee, who asked not to be identified.

"We wanted a coach that was clean and dedicated to academics. We wanted a coach that could recruit and win championships. And we wanted a coach that could get along with the public and the press. We've had enough of what the other guy [Perkins] has done."

In Curry, the committee seemed to find all of the ingredients.

In an era in which greed and corruption dominate the sports headlines, Curry is one of those rare individuals who stands for what is right.

Who can forget Curry's decision to suspend his starting senior quarterback at last year's All American Bowl for missing curfew?

Aside from Penn State's Joe Paterno, it's hard to find a coach in college football with the kind of respect and integrity as Alabama's new man.

It's also hard to find many schools that will hire two consecutive head coaches with losing records.

Curry's 31-43-4 record is a slight improvement on Perkins's 24-35 record with the New York Giants. Perkins had one winning season in four and a trip to the playoffs. Curry has had two winning seasons in seven and a single bowl trip.

This year, he went 5-5-1. The tie was to Furman, and one of the losses was to Wake Forest.

Incredibly, Fred Akers was fired recently at Texas after winning 75 percent of his games. Ted Tollner went to the Rose and Citrus bowls in four years at USC but was fired because he couldn't beat Notre Dame and UCLA.

Certainly it's not hard to make a case that Curry has had a lousy record.

A seven-year record of 31-43-4 is nothing to be proud of. And you can bet Auburn fans are circling the Iron Bowl on the calendar. Curry is 0-7 against the Tigers.

Still, it's unlikely the kind of bitter hatred that developed between Perkins and Pat Dye before last year's Iron Bowl will continue.

"I don't think you have to hate anybody, but you sure need to get ready to whip them," Curry said, referring to Auburn.

However, the big story yesterday wasn't Bill Curry. It was Joab Thomas.

The Alabama president has set a new standard. Now it will be interesting to see if anyone follows.

While Auburn was led by an All-American running back who probably wouldn't know what the inside of the library looks like, Alabama has chosen a man who values academics as ferverently as winning.

It's a nice change.

If I ever did a top-ten list of barf-bag columns, this one would be No. 1. But it just shows the cunning and cleverness of Bill Curry. And to steal a phrase from the column a few days earlier about the comment from P. T. Barnum, the sucker this time was looking me in the mirror.

MARCH 27, 1987

Confrontation with Knight isn't so bad

It was a typical dreary winter morning in Bloomington, Indiana. The sky was gray, the ground covered with snow.

But inside Assembly Hall, basketball fever kept everyone warm. Everyone but this reporter, who had chills running down his spine.

It was 9:50. In ten minutes, I had an appointment to interview Bobby Knight, the basketball coach at Indiana University.

It was 1981, and UAB was to meet the Hoosiers the following night in the semifinals of the Mideast Regional.

A few days earlier, my (former) boss thought it would be a good idea to call ahead and set up an interview with Knight.

"No way he'll talk to me," I told my boss, figuring he would tell me to go visit Gene Bartow instead.

"He might," replied the bossman, who happened to be from Indiana. Score one for the Hoosier.

"Just be at his office at 10 a.m.," said Knight's publicity man when I called for the interview.

So here I was, in the outer lobby of the basketball office, about to interview the General.

Only one problem.

"I'm sorry," his secretary said when I gave her my name. "But I don't show you having an appointment this morning with Coach Knight."

"You must be mistaken," I said.

No mistake, she said.

So I whipped around the corner to go visit the fellow who had set it up.

"I forgot to tell him," he said in a voice that told me he actually had been afraid to ask.

The newspaper was expecting a Bobby Knight story, and I had to figure out a way to come up with one. The boss might have understood under normal circumstances. But since I had boasted to everyone with an ear about my scheduled interview, I was in big trouble.

So when Knight walked out of his office a few minutes later, I jumped him. Not like he jumped the Puerto Rican policeman during the Pan American Games, but something like that.

I explained the situation. He didn't say a word. He just stared.

"I drove 1,000 miles up here to talk to you," I told him, expecting a brush off.

"What do you want?" Knight barked.

"Well ... uh ... uh ..." I said. "Well ... uh ... I want to interview you."

"So what do you want?" he said again.

At this point, I realized he wasn't going to offer me a chair (I was afraid he might throw one) and a cup of espresso.

I would love to report to you that it was the greatest interview I've ever had.

It wasn't.

But it was nice of him to talk to me. And for some reason, I've always liked him just a little bit more as a result.

It is very fashionable for sportswriters to knock Bobby Knight. It is easy to say he has no class, that he curses too much.

Both criticisms are correct.

But he does a lot of good things. If you don't believe it, talk to former players and coaches.

Or read *A Season on the Brink*, the extraordinary bestseller by John Feinstein.

In the book, Feinstein shows the explosive tirades and mental manipulation of his players. But he also describes the other side of the coach that few see, but more ought to.

I really don't care if Indiana beats UNLV tomorrow in the Final Four. I quit caring about the NCAA Tournament when Providence beat Austin Peay.

But I'll be watching Bob Knight tomorrow afternoon. It's hard not to.

I've also been reading him lately. Some newspapers (not us, but hey, we had enough with Sanderson, Smith, and Bartow) are running Knight's column this month.

He is not much of a writer, although don't expect him to agree with that.

"People are payin' for this thing," he said, referring to the columns. "Those papers are paying me $250 or $300 for those six columns.

"It takes me about four minutes to write a column. Twelve minutes into three columns a week. That's about $20 a minute. Hell, I might quit coaching for that."

But the best words involving Knight this season have not been written by him—but about him.

On the last page of *A Season on the Brink*, Feinstein describes the coach this way:

"He has so much to give—and has given so much. And when he begins his 22nd season as a college coach this fall, he will only be 46 years old. A young man with a bright future. If he doesn't destroy it."

On second thought, if I were a basketball coach, I would probably be like Bobby Knight. I have always had a fetish for throwing chairs.

September 28, 1987

In do-or-die situation, Dye finds way to die

Once again, a big game was on the line Saturday—one that had both national championship and Southeastern Conference title implications.

Once again, Auburn coach Pat Dye found a way to blow it.

So what else is new?

Over the years, Dye's choking in big games has become as dependable as the autumn foliage. Maybe one day it will change. But there will probably be a cure for AIDS before it does.

There is no sense going through all the soiled details of Auburn's 20-20 tie with Tennessee. By now, you probably are aware that Auburn had a 10-point lead with 11 minutes left in the game. That's when Auburn's vaunted defense, one many people have called the best in the country, was ripped apart like red meat by a mad dog.

Tennessee drove 55 yards for a field goal, then 56 yards for the tying touchdown.

Then the 93,506 spectators at Neyland Stadium, plus a national television audience, got to view "The Pat Dye Comedy Show" on the sidelines. This time, his trusted assistant, Pat Sullivan, played a costarring role.

Coaches spend all year working on this situation, which makes it more difficult to understand how Dye and his staff continue to find ways to blow the big games.

"That's life," Dye said.

The season isn't over. But Auburn's chances of winning the SEC title might be.

There is a good chance someone, perhaps LSU, will go through the league schedule undefeated. Even Tennessee, with an easy schedule remaining (Alabama, Ole Miss, Vanderbilt, Kentucky) has a chance, which might be why Johnny Majors made his controversial decision to go for a tie.

There might have been other reasons, too. These days, Majors has a lot on his mind.

Insiders say a national magazine has just concluded a lengthy investigation into Majors's recruiting practices at Tennessee. It's believed the magazine will expose a "major scandal" at Tennessee in its upcoming issue, expected to hit the streets shortly.

But none of that should have affected Dye, who two years ago tried to blame the Knoxville press for helping the Vols get ready. As a result, he closed practice last week to reporters.

Maybe he didn't want the laughter from the media to interrupt his workout. It would be hard to control oneself watching Dye and his assistant trying to coach the two-minute offense.

It certainly was funny to watch Saturday in a live game.

But it isn't fair to say Dye never wins the big game. Last year, the Tigers upset Alabama in the Iron Bowl. If Dye had his way, however, Auburn would have called a timeout instead of allowing Lawyer Tillman to run a reverse and score.

Perhaps Dye will shed some more light on the Tennessee game today when he comes to Birmingham to speak to the Monday Morning Quarterback Club.

Since Dye has done his best to take all of Auburn's football games out of Birmingham, one hopes he will remember how to get here.

In case you've forgotten, Coach Dye, Birmingham is the city with all the buildings off I-65 between Montgomery and Huntsville.

There were probably some Alabama fans who were ready to send Bill Curry a road map back to Atlanta late Saturday night.

Things were looking grim for Curry and Alabama until Bobby Humphrey saved the Tide from a humiliating evening.

You have to hand it to Curry. He coached his team to a victory over a school that narrowly lost to Duke, which lost Saturday to traditional powerhouse Virginia 42-17.

One thing Curry apparently didn't do was get his team's attention following the Florida whipping. When you have to come back with last-minute heroics to beat a team such as Vanderbilt, it doesn't bode well when you are looking ahead at Tennessee, LSU, Notre Dame, and Auburn.

Perhaps Curry just made the mistake last week of looking ahead. Southwestern Louisiana is next for the Crimson Tide.

Judging by the Tide's performance against lowly Vanderbilt, anybody might be capable of giving Alabama a tough game.

The Auburn-Tennessee game in Knoxville every other year usually provided me with some of my best material. This year was no exception.

OCTOBER 12, 1987

Curry's honeymoon ends abruptly with incomprehensible loss

MEMPHIS—Following each of the past four games, Alabama coach Bill Curry has discussed his team's inept performance with promises and guarantees that mistakes would be reduced.

But so far, Curry's gift of prophecy is no better than his overall coaching record, which now stands at 35-45-4.

It is safe to say that Curry's honeymoon at Alabama ended here Saturday in one of the most shocking and embarrassing upsets in the school's storied football tradition.

Should it happen again, a number of Alabama fans might want to begin divorce proceedings against the first-year coach.

Certainly, there would be a market for "Let's Get Rid of Curry in a Hurry" bumper stickers.

People can understand losses to Florida. They don't like it. But they understand it.

But a loss to Memphis State is difficult to comprehend.

Before Saturday, Memphis State had only won three football games out of its past thirty. This is a school that drew only 16,330 for its season finale last year.

But on Saturday in a 65,000-seat stadium, 40,622 fans paid to watch the home team play one of the (former) big names in college football. Some 13,000 of those fans wore Crimson.

Of course, the small turnout was a break for Curry. Can you imagine the laughter had the game been played in Birmingham, or been broadcast on television?

There would have been laughter because Alabama's performance against Memphis State was a joke. A bad one at that.

A few weeks ago, some Alabama fans thought the loss of quarterback David Smith was a break for the Tide. They viewed it as a chance for Curry to play one of three former high school All-Americans on the bench. But so far, Smith's injury has proved to be very costly.

As limited as Smith was, he was superior to anything Alabama has played since.

Curry has yet to find a new quarterback. When you consider the seventh game of the season is upon us, it makes you wonder what he has been doing with his time.

Curry is known as one of the finest orators and motivators in the game. Members of the Board of Trustees said Curry's style was one of the key reasons they were sold on him for the job.

Unfortunately, none of this appears to have rubbed off on his team.

Instead of playing inspired football, his team has resembled the Keystone Cops in critical situations.

Some people point to the young players as part of the problem.

"We have to show more leadership and the younger guys have to mature and help us win," Alabama cornerback Gene Jelks said. "I think some of them are young and inexperienced, and when they get in certain situations, they panic and are really not conscious of what they are doing.

"It can be critical and it hurts."

Curry agreed with Jelks.

"We just have to go out there with a different level of commitment. You can't do it with talk. You can't do it talking on the radio or writing in the newspaper or standing in front of a group of people yelling and screaming. Somehow, you've got to get the players focused on what we're about here."

That's nice to know, but why isn't it being done? Isn't that what Curry and his staff are being paid big money to do?

There was no excuse for Alabama to lose on Saturday. Twice, the Crimson Tide was inside the 6-yard line and failed to get any points. Too many times, it made costly penalties, one holding call costing the Tide the winning touchdown.

At the moment, this program appears to be in chaos. You can blame the players. You can say Bobby Humphrey's mysterious leg cramps have hurt the Tide badly down the stretch.

But we all know at whose feet the blame should be placed.

"To blame anybody else but me would be a cop-out," Curry said.

It might be overly optimistic to say Alabama still has a chance this season, but there is talent on this team.

Considering the magnitude of this upset, I always regretted not having been tougher on Curry in this piece. However, I worked assiduously to make up for my mistake.

NOVEMBER 16, 1987

Tide at loss for words after losing respect

SOUTH BEND, Indiana—The sun had slipped over the horizon, turning the warmth of a glorious November afternoon into a cold, dark evening. And high above in the stillness of the Indiana sky, you could see the view from the Golden Dome, the centerpiece of this fabled campus.

It was a marvelous sight, just like the scene a few blocks away at Notre Dame Stadium, where the Fighting Irish and Alabama had just finished their little war.

Although the game had been over for almost 10 minutes, nobody was leaving. The fans remained, cheering for the Notre Dame seniors, who were thanking the student body for their support.

They had seen Notre Dame punish Alabama 37-6, and now they were reaping the spoils of victory.

When the last senior had spoken, the band began playing that familiar tune.

"Cheer, cheer for old Notre Dame ... wake up the echoes cheering her name ... ."

It was an extraordinary moment, the kind Chris Schenkel used to say "makes college football the great game it is."

For once, he was right.

But a few yards away, beneath the rocking stadium, the only sound that could be heard was silence.

As the Alabama players dressed, hardly a word was uttered. The talking had been done on the field.

In Alabama's case, it was barely a whimper.

The Crimson Tide had come to this bedrock of college football to lay its claim for greatness. Instead, it was humiliated beyond belief.

Not only in front of the 58,000 fans in Notre Dame Stadium, but in front of millions of television viewers.

Coach Bill Curry, who must shoulder the blame, was trying to come up with an explanation. Those eyes, which seemed to be on temporary loan from Ray Perkins, peered straight ahead.

"We were beaten, no, we got whipped and whipped good by a much better football team," Curry said. "We just got whipped. I can't say it any clearer."

Then, Curry proceeded to rattle off a handful of reasons, as if he were reading from an old script.

The fact that Alabama lost here really is not surprising. First of all, it is difficult to follow an emotional victory such as LSU. Great teams find a way. But Alabama is clearly not a great team.

However, there was no excuse for an Alabama football team to be mishandled as this team was.

Losing 37-6 is what happens to teams such as Louisville and Kansas. Not to Alabama.

But this is not an ordinary Alabama team. This is a team that lost to Florida, which lost to Georgia, which was destroyed by Auburn. It is a team that lost to Memphis State, which was butchered by Southwestern Louisiana.

Suddenly, the thrill of victories over Penn State and Tennessee and LSU has been washed away. In its place, the sour, putrid morning aftertaste of defeat.

However, as every Alabama fan knows, and as Brent Musburger put so well on CBS:

"But all will be forgiven if Alabama can beat Auburn. Believe me, it is that important. But nothing will be forgiven if he (Curry) doesn't win that one."

Musburger might be a Yankee, but he's been to Alabama. He knows what's important here.

Early indications are Auburn will be roughly a 3½-point favorite over the Crimson Tide. It could go higher. But until Saturday in South Bend, Alabama always had proved the Las Vegas bookies wrong.

But not this Saturday, this black day in Alabama history. Bear Bryant never could beat Notre Dame. But he never lost by 31 points, either.

So what happens next?

"Right now I don't have any comments on Auburn," Alabama cornerback Gene Jelks said. "No comment."

Curry had cautioned his players not to "shoot their mouths off" about Auburn.

"I don't want to hear a bunch of 'we gonnas' from them," Curry said.

"Preparing for this kind of game in state does not include shooting your mouth off. That kind of thing ends up on bulletin boards, you know."

When Curry finished his answer, there was one final question.

"How about the bowl matchups?"

"I don't know," Curry said. "I'm not worried about bowls. Right now, we better get our act together and be ready to play Auburn University."

Hopefully, for Alabama fans, Curry will do a better job preparing his team for Auburn than he did against Notre Dame.

He certainly couldn't do any worse.

This was one of the most unforgettable trips I've made as a sportswriter. I have been back once, and it is a place every college football fan needs to visit. Maybe some of you can go visit when UAB becomes Notre Dame's annual homecoming opponent.

March 17, 1988

He was a good coach, and he was good

ATLANTA—On the floor of the Omni, basketballs were bouncing off the hardwood as coach Sonny Smith and his Auburn Tigers prepared for today's first-round NCAA Tournament game against Bradley.

Just another day in the world of sports.

But all of a sudden, at least for me, the sound of basketballs stopped.

Someone ran up to me and asked: "Have you heard the news?"

"What news?"

"Rollie Dotsch. He died."

I started to call the office to see if it was true. But I put the phone down.

I knew it was.

Rollie Dotsch, who coached the Birmingham Stallions throughout their history in the defunct U.S. Football League, had been dying for some time.

Only four days ago, someone had called to say Dotsch had taken a turn for the worse. The end was near.

And now, as I looked out into the empty arena in this cold city, suddenly basketball didn't seem very important.

It didn't matter anymore that Hersey Hawkins, Bradley's All-American guard, was about to speak at a press conference a few yards away.

It only mattered that Rollie Dotsch was gone.

Suddenly, I began to think back to all the times I had spent with him, the countless plane rides, the dinners and football games.

I remembered when we met.

And the last time we saw each other.

There are many wonderful memories of this man who touched so many in our community.

He was a kind man. But he also was a football coach. He could be as tough as nails.

I'll never forget a trip to Detroit in 1983. Dotsch was determined to pay back the Michigan kicker, Novo Bojovic, who had beaten the Stallions a few weeks earlier and then taunted some of the Birmingham players.

As we hung around that the hotel that morning, Dotsch said, "Watch opening kickoff tonight."

I did. I saw a Stallions player smash into the kicker. Bojovic was shaken, so much that he blew a short field goal try at the end of the game, ensuring the Stallions' victory.

I didn't like what I had seen and told Dotsch so on the plane ride home.

Dotsch put his arm around me and said, "Son, this is not a game for women and children. Those guys aren't wearing skirts out there. They're wearing uniforms."

He was a football coach. A pretty good one, too. He was selected USFL Coach of the Year in 1985.

In the final months of the USFL—while the only action was done by attorneys—Dotsch still showed up for work. There was little to do, but he always put on a happy face.

One December morning in 1986, when I read a story over the Associated Press wire that Dan Henning had been fired as coach of the Atlanta Falcons, I called Dotsch immediately. I knew he wanted the job badly.

"Good morning, Birmingham Stallions," came the voice over the phone.

"Is that you, Rollie?" I asked.

"That's right," he said. "I'm wearing the secretary's skirt today."

He went to Atlanta a few weeks later for an interview. But the job went to Marion Campbell.

There was talk for a while that Dotsch might become UAB's first football coach. Athletic director Gene Bartow wanted Dotsch for the job, but the school never went through with starting a football program.

Finally, last spring, Dotsch took a job with the Minnesota Vikings as an assistant coach.

It was there last summer that he discovered he had pancreatic cancer.

For months, Dotsch's friends in Birmingham wondered about him. Finally, in November, he came back for a weekend to see old friends and players.

One afternoon, while he was in town, I went to see him for an interview. When he answered the hotel door, my heart sank.

It was like seeing a ghost. Dotsch had lost 60 pounds. I bit my lip and told him how good he looked.

He smiled.

"I've been trying to lose weight for a long time," he said. "I finally did."

For two hours we talked about his illness.

I tried to be upbeat. I told him he could lick the disease.

He shook his head.

"The odds aren't very good."

When he said that I began to feel sick. What was I doing here, with a pencil and notebook in my hand?

There is a time and place for everything. But for me this was not the time for a newspaper story.

"Rollie, do you really want this to come out in the paper?"

He shook his head.

"Not really."

I put up my notebook. We talked a few more minutes, and I got up to leave.

I shook his hand, knowing it would be for the last time. Then, he hugged me.

"I really appreciate you not writing about this now," Dotsch said. "You can use it when I'm gone."

A very tough column to write about a wonderful man.

JUNE 13, 1988

Perkins softens stance (if only just a little bit)

Often in this business, you read stories about the day in the life of a famous politician or sports figure. This one is about me. It happened last Saturday.

5:45 a.m.—My alarm clock just went off, and I feel lousy. My head is splitting (even though I don't drink). This day is going to be different. I'm about to spend time with a man I really don't like.

His name is Ray Perkins.

You may have heard of him.

To some, that may not be a big deal.

But it is to me. You see, Perkins and I are about as close as Nancy Reagan and Raisa Gorbachev.

But he was coming to town for the Rollie Dotsch tournament, and I thought he'd make a good guest for the Saturday morning radio show I do on WAPI-AM with John Forney.

I called Perkins. Incredibly, he agreed to be on the show.

7:42 a.m.—I have eaten a good breakfast (just in case Perkins and I get into a fight). As I pull into the Ramada Civic Center Hotel to pick him up, he is waiting, cup of coffee in his hand. I wonder if he is going to splatter me with it.

Instead, Perkins extends his hand. We exchange greetings. Typically, the first thing we talk about is the weather. After four years of cold war silence between us, Perkins and I are talking about relative humidity and ground clutter. Where is Mike Royer when you really need him?

7:48 a.m.—The conversation has turned to Alabama football, thank goodness. I mention the changes Steve Sloan and Bill Curry have made, many of them undoing things he had done.

At first, he ignores the question. But then, he answers, saying he's happy Forney is back. But he still doesn't understand why Paul Kennedy got the ax.

"I haven't figured what Paul did (wrong). Paul did a good job, was very professional. But everybody has got their own way."

7:51 a.m.—We're still in my car, driving through a deserted downtown. I ask him about Curry and what it takes to win at Alabama. He looks at me with a stern look. It's obvious Perkins is about to say something very important.

"I do know one thing," he said. "I think the one ingredient that it takes to be the head coach at the University of Alabama, one ingredient that you must possess (is) you have got to be a tough son-of-a-bitch."

Perkins goes silent when asked if Curry has the right ingredient.

"The most important thing is winning," he finally says.

8:05 a.m.—The small talk is over. It's show time. It gets off to a miserable start.

I try to joke with Perkins about all of his titles at Tampa Bay (vice-president, general manager, and head coach), asking him if I've missed something.

"It really doesn't matter, Paul," he shoots back.

Ooh, that hurt.

Maybe, I should have invited another guest. Perhaps, SEC commish Harvey Schiller could have been on, talking about how to write a résumé.

It doesn't get any better with the next question. I ask him about the first season at Tampa, which was marred by the NFL strike.

"I didn't cause the strike now," he said. "You're not blaming that on me."

Maybe, Perkins hasn't changed at all.

8:13 a.m.—We are in commercial. The telephone console is lit up like a Christmas tree with callers wanting to talk with Perkins. But Perkins informs me he doesn't want to take calls.

"The callers put me in a frame of mind I don't like to be in," he says. "It doesn't take but two or three questions to really get me in a bad mood."

Perkins said he was planning to cancel his own radio show if he had stayed at Alabama even though he made $35,000 from it.

"They offered me about twice that in Tampa Bay. I told them I wasn't interested."

I thought how nice it must be to be rich enough to turn down $75,000.

8:20 a.m.—The discussion turns to Homer Smith, Alabama's offensive coordinator. Smith recently said one of Alabama's problems last year was a lack of experience at quarterback. Perkins is asked if he takes responsibility because he didn't play anyone but Mike Shula.

"There you go accusing me again," Perkins responds sharply. "How can I take any responsibility if I'm not there. That's ludicrous."

He also refuses to evaluate Jeff Dunn, Vince Sutton, and David Smith, all of whom he recruited. Perkins said he had a starter picked out for the following year, but declines to name him.

"It wouldn't be fair."

8:31 a.m.—The subject returns to Curry. How long should he be given? "It's not an overnight deal," he said. "It takes two years to get your program implemented. I think the third and fourth year is when you start playing with your recruits. That's when you accurately measure the type of job a coach is doing."

8:35 a.m.—I ask him if he had it to do over, would he have done things differently.

Perkins said he would have fired everyone the first day and started from scratch. His two most difficult firings: Forney and Ken Donahue.

8:40 a.m.—The segment is almost over. But I couldn't resist bringing up a statement made just six days before his resignation. Asked by a reporter if he was leaving for Tampa Bay, Perkins responded:

"I'm going to be at Alabama for a long time. I'd say the odds of me leaving are a million to one."

Why did you say that?

"I remember somebody asking me: 'Is it a million to one?' and I think probably agreed with him just to get out of the room, because I have had my times when I really would rather not be in the same room with writers or radio announcers."

I thought for a moment about that statement. I have felt the same way about football coaches—especially Ray Perkins.

But not this day. Suddenly, things were different. Ray Perkins and I will never be good friends. But the bitterness of yesterday was no longer there.

Like most things in life, it too had passed.

My partner, Bob Lochamy, had called Perkins's office on a lark. Surprisingly, he agreed to be on the show. I was extremely nervous picking him considering we had not spoken in some time. But the meeting changed my opinion of Perkins (at least, for a day).

September 19, 1988

Tide's Sloan out to lunch when storm hit

COLLEGE STATION, Texas—While the debate continues over Bill Curry's decision to postpone the Alabama-Texas A&M game [due to Hurricane Gilbert], a bigger question seems to have gone unanswered.

At the Democratic National Convention in July, many people asked the question of Vice President George Bush: "Where was George?"

Considering the embarrassing decision by Curry last Friday, a similar question might be asked: "Where was Steve?"

Steve Sloan, that is, who sometimes (though usually not in times of crisis) is athletic director at the University of Alabama.

When push came to shove last Friday, Sloan seemed to be hiding under a desk seeking shelter from the storm.

Who says?

Among others, his former roommate at Alabama: Jackie Sherrill.

Sherrill, the head coach and athletic director at Texas A&M, said over the weekend that Sloan was in favor of Alabama playing the game Saturday.

"He's just sick about this," Sherrill said.

When Sherrill tried to talk him out of the decision to cancel, Sloan passed the buck to Curry.

"But you're the athletic director," Sherrill said.

It didn't matter.

Curry is not paid to make these type of decisions at Alabama. That's what the athletic director is supposed to do. But Sloan apparently was spineless when faced with, perhaps, his most important decision at Alabama.

When Harry Truman was in the White House, he had a sign on his desk that read: "The buck stops here."

An appropriate sign for Sloan's office might be: "Out to lunch." Because that's where he seemed to be last Friday when decisions had to be made.

As a result, the image of Alabama football has taken a more severe beating than the Texas coast did from Hurricane Gilbert.

On ESPN, jokes were made about Alabama all afternoon Saturday. ESPN commentator Lee Corso, who formerly coached at Indiana, quipped: "Let me tell you something: If I had known it was so easy to cancel games when I was coaching, I would have never gone to Lincoln or Baton Rouge or Columbus, Ohio."

In the *Houston Chronicle* yesterday, columnist Al Carter asked: "Has the Crimson Tide become the Yellow Tide?"

Carter referred to the Alabama coach as "Bill Scurry." Some Aggie fans talked of a new poultry cuisine: "Chicken Curry."

Others joked that the only damage fans sustained by coming to College Station this weekend was skin cancer from too much sun.

Yesterday, in Tuscaloosa, Sloan found no humor from any of this. The soft-spoken and likable athletic director chose his words carefully when asked who made the controversial decision.

"It was a collective decision," Sloan said, "but primarily, it was his [Curry's], since the team is his responsibility."

Sloan was asked why he didn't make the decision himself.

"I think when people's lives are involved, the decision should lie with the coach who recruited these people, who talked to their family and deals with them on a daily basis."

Based on that assumption, two lives of little or no value to Alabama were associate athletic director Tommy Limbaugh and assistant athletic director Steve Townsend. Sloan sent the school plane into College Station Friday afternoon to bring the two men home. Both made it safely.

Although Sloan is said to have sharply disagreed with Curry's decision, he would not comment yesterday.

"It would not be productive for me to comment on that," Sloan said. But he quickly added, "I support the decision."

The last few days have been a trying time for Alabama. I hope the storm will pass and calm will return. But a serious question remains: Who is running the Alabama athletic department?

Meanwhile, the Crimson Tide heads back to the practice field this afternoon to prepare for Saturday's home game against Vanderbilt.

Weather permitting.

One had to know this was the beginning of the end for Sloan and Curry. Regardless, I had a wonderful weekend in College Station, hanging out with Texas A&M coach Jackie Sherrill, eating free food, watching college football, and trashing Curry—and not necessarily in that order.

DECEMBER 17, 1988

Limbaugh beats the bushes for talent

TUSCALOOSA—Behind Tommy Limbaugh's desk at the University of Alabama, a sign reads, "Recruiting is just like shaving. You have to do it every day or you look like a bum."

Limbaugh knows the feeling well. For 12 of his 44 years, Limbaugh has been a recruiting coordinator at Texas Tech, Ole Miss, and Duke. And now, at Alabama.

Bill Curry, the Alabama football coach, has said, "He's the best recruiter in the country."

But when Limbaugh followed Steve Sloan to Alabama from Duke nearly two years ago, he retired his title.

He became the associate athletic director at Alabama, considered by some to be "the most powerful man in the school's athletic department."

But two weeks ago, fearing a disaster in the recruiting wars because of uncertainty in the program, Curry called his old friend back to service, putting him in charge of signing high school prospects. Although it was a temporary post, Limbaugh's wife, Marcia, was not impressed.

"She didn't talk to me for a week," Limbaugh said.

The reason was simple. Recruiters never stop recruiting. And they almost never see their families.

The following is the story of one day in a recruiter's life. It happened last Wednesday.

5:19 a.m. CST—On the radio, a disc jockey is screaming. Even at this hour, they don't know how to talk.

"It's 5:19, 19 minutes after five," he said. "The temperature is a nippy 31 degrees."

In the black of night, Tommy Limbaugh is shivering. He's also mad. Limbaugh is supposed to leave for an all-day recruiting trip in 11 minutes. So far, no sign of the plane.

5:47 a.m. CST—Finally, the peaceful sound of morning is broken with the landing of a small Lear jet. Normally, Limbaugh would take the school plane. But it's broken.

On the horizon, the first sign of day has arrived.

6:18 a.m. CST—Limbaugh takes off his camel-hair jacket as the plane takes off. He does not loosen his blue tie. He hasn't been in the office for two weeks. There is much work to do on the plane.

7:56 a.m. EST—Outside the window below, there is a spectacular view of the Smoky Mountains. Limbaugh looks out for a moment but is more interested in a Christmas card from his daughter, Leslie. She is a freshman at Duke.

8:38 a.m. EST—A familiar sight can be seen below—the Washington Monument. Not far away, one can see the U.S. Capitol. Limbaugh doesn't even look up. High school signing date is Feb. 8. This is no time for sightseeing.

9:26 a.m. EST—Welcome to Philadelphia, City of Brotherly Love. It is 25 degrees. The wind chill brings it down to 15. Limbaugh stops to rent a car.

In a minute, Limbaugh is driving down the interstate. He goes past Veteran's Stadium where Alabama opened the 1988 season against Temple. Much has happened since then.

Across the Walt Whitman Bridge into New Jersey, there is no welcome sign telling you where you are. All you have to do is roll down the window and breathe.

Why, Limbaugh is asked, do you have to recruit in New Jersey?

"We don't do much recruiting here," Limbaugh said. "Our philosophy is to dominate the state of Alabama. We only go outside Alabama for a kid who is a difference maker."

He is 45 minutes away from one of those.

10:10 a.m. EST—Limbaugh is getting close. This will be the first of the allowed six visits college recruiters can make to a player. Face-to-face visits begin Dec. 1. One of those can be made by the head coach. NCAA rules state only one visit a week. Of course, the prospect can make an official visit to the campus. The player Limbaugh is about to visit came last weekend. Limbaugh likes to follow it up immediately with a return visit.

It is the culmination of almost a year of work. Initial contact starts in the player's junior year. Letters are sent out to all of the top prospects. The winnowing process begins.

"You have to make smart decisions," Limbaugh said. Some believe Alabama has not done enough of this since Curry arrived.

To some people, recruiting is more important than the season. Numerous recruiting publications are on the market. It dominates radio talk shows this time of the year. Some people fear it has replaced college basketball as winter's dominant sport in the South.

There are all types of recruiting. Negative recruiting is a favorite. Players often receive newspaper articles with no return address. If someone writes a negative article about Curry, you can bet a recruit will see it.

"If they are doing that to people I'm recruiting," Limbaugh said, "it will work against them. I won't say why. But it will."

10:21 a.m. EST—Limbaugh pulls his car in front of the high school. It has a steeple with an old clock on top. It looks more New England than New Jersey.

Limbaugh introduces himself at the school office. As he asks for the head coach, a teacher walks in.

"It's a good thing you got here now," the man tells Limbaugh.

"Why is that?"

"Auburn just called."

Limbaugh's eyebrows raise.

The man laughs.

Limbaugh realizes it was a joke.

10:43 a.m. EST—Limbaugh is in the guidance counselor's office, checking the player's transcripts. (To avoid any conflicts with NCAA policy, no names of players or high schools will be used in this story.)

Limbaugh looks concerned. If one had to bet, this kid Limbaugh is about to visit will be a Proposition 48 player.

10:49 a.m. EST—The head coach has been found. He and Limbaugh now go looking for the kid. This is no ordinary kid.

He is a 6-foot-6, 265-pound defensive lineman. Some say he is the best in the country. He has a 32-inch waist.

While he finishes a test in gym class, Limbaugh talks to the coach.

"What is he thinking about?" Limbaugh asks.

"If he had to make a decision right now, I think he would choose Alabama," the coach replies." Of course, he doesn't have to. He gets three more visits."

He has been to Michigan State and Alabama. He hasn't decided between UCLA, Nebraska, Tennessee, Florida State, and Ohio State for the remainder of the visits.

Some schools don't want him because of his grades. Alabama will take him regardless.

11:01 a.m. EST—The prospect has arrived. He looks like an All-American. Tall and muscular and very thin.

"Did you enjoy your visit?" Limbaugh asks.

"I really did," the kid says. "That (basketball) game was definitely exciting. When I visited with the head coach, I felt like I was part of the family. That's what I didn't have at Michigan State. I felt more at home. Life is slower, but that's not all bad."

"Hey," said Limbaugh, "If we can sign you, I'll get to eat for another year."

The kid laughs.

Limbaugh talks about the prospect's cousin, who plays basketball for Alabama. Limbaugh said he can room with his cousin.

The kid shakes his head.

Now, Limbaugh goes into *the pitch.*

"Alabama has won 11 national championships. So if winning is important, go to a school where they have tradition. Nobody else has won more. Now, I don't know about Russia."

The kid laughs again. Limbaugh is on a roll. And he knows it.

"The most (national championships) anybody else from the South has won is one," Limbaugh said, mentioning Ole Miss, LSU, Auburn, Georgia, and Tennessee. "Alabama has also won more football games than anybody since 1923.

"How many bowl games do you think Alabama has been to in the last 30 years?"

The kid guesses 16.

"In the last 30 years, Alabama has been to 29."

That impresses both the kid and the coach.

"At Alabama, the sky is the limit," Limbaugh said. "You better come to Alabama with one objective—to win the national championship."

Limbaugh also mentions academics.

"The worst thing that will happen to you at Alabama is you'll graduate."

Now that's a line.

The coach mentions that some schools have tried to cheat and he doesn't like it.

Like a politician, Limbaugh sees an opening.

"Don't let it happen," Limbaugh said, raising his voice. "That is selling your soul. It not worth it for a few thousand dollars or a car. You are selling your soul for the rest of your life. Someone asked me earlier if Alabama did that. I told him Alabama has won 11 national championships. We never cheated."

Limbaugh looks at the kid and leans forward.

"Please don't let somebody own you like a slave. The school that does that does not care about an individual. All they care about it winning."

It is time to go. As the player, head coach, and Limbaugh walk out the door, a male teacher stops them.

"Don't listen to all that bull ... about Alabama," he tells the kid. "Go to Maryland."

Limbaugh grins and says "I thought they were going to give up football."

Everybody laughs. It has been a good visit.

12:25 p.m. EST—Back in Philadelphia. Limbaugh calls his secretary. Then he boards the jet. He nibbles on a turkey sandwich the pilot has left for him. In this business, there is no such thing as a lunch hour.

1:12 p.m. EST—As the plane begins its final descent into Syracuse, New York, Limbaugh looks out the window. The ground is covered with snow.

"It looks like we're flying into the North Pole at Christmas," Limbaugh says. The temperature in Syracuse is 24 degrees. With the wind chill, it is near zero. Bone-chilling cold.

Limbaugh is met by a man in his early forties. He played at Alabama 20 years ago. A walk-on. He will drive Limbaugh to the high school.

1:58 p.m. EST—The driveway at the high school is covered with ice. Limbaugh is careful not to slip. Before he gets to the school office, a man rushes up to him.

"Hey," he says, smugly, "Notre Dame is in with him right now. Penn State has already been here once today to talk to him."

Him is one of the top running backs in America. The player has been picked for the *Parade* All-America team. During the season, he scored 50 points in a game (seven touchdowns, for 2-point conversions).

First, Limbaugh talks to the head coach. The head coach stuns everyone with his next statement.

The coach was born in *Auburn.* Not Auburn, New York, some 35 miles to the west. But Auburn, Alabama, as in the Loveliest Village on the Plains.

Someone jokes about last year's Sugar Bowl. People here in Syracuse are still bitter over the 16-16 tie that ruined the Orangemen's perfect season.

"I still pull for Auburn," the coach says after Limbaugh gets out of ear range. "I went back there in February to bury my grandfather."

One gets the feeling this could be a tough visit.

The kid walks in. He looks good. He stands 6-2 and weighs 205. He has 4.5 speed in the 40-yard dash.

Limbaugh starts in, telling the kid about Alabama's tradition and the bowl games and the national championships and the television appearances. And the academics.

"The worst thing that will happen to you at Alabama is you'll graduate."

Limbaugh asks the prospect what he wants from a school.

The prospect said he wants a good offensive line.

"What else?"

"A good coaching staff," said the player. Before Limbaugh can say anything, the player adds, "That's going to be there the whole time that I'm there."

The question has finally come up. The one about Bill Curry's future.

"Who can guarantee that?" Limbaugh said.

"I don't know," said the kid.

"I don't know who can guarantee that," Limbaugh said. "I believe that our administration, our Board of Trustees, has made a strong statement on national television that Bill Curry is going to be here the remainder of his contract. I would sort of eliminate that from your thinking."

The coach shows no emotion. He looks bored.

"When you pick a school, you should pick a school," Limbaugh continued.

He begins to talk about the past season.

"We finished 8-3. That's not good. That's a bad season for Alabama."

Of course, Limbaugh doesn't mention it was better than last year's 7-5 record.

"But we're this close," said Limbaugh, putting his two fingers about an inch apart, "from being an 11-0 team."

Limbaugh moves a little closer to the kid.

"What if we had you? What if we had you at tailback against Auburn. Could you make the difference? You're a difference-type player, you know that, don't you?

"In your heart, you know. You're one guy that we didn't have this year. If we did, we're probably 11-0 and fighting for the national championship."

The meeting is over. To win this kid, Alabama must beat UCLA, Notre Dame, and hometown Syracuse.

It could be tougher for Bill Curry than beating Auburn.

4:03 p.m. EST—After spending 45 minutes returning calls at the airport hangar, Limbaugh boards the plane. It's time to head south. On the plane, Limbaugh shuts his eyes for about 10 minutes. He slept three hours the night before. But as the plane flies over Pittsburgh, he is back at work.

4:40 p.m. CST—To the west, the sun is slipping over the horizon. Still the orange and red hues make a spectacular sight. In the other direction, it is black.

"We're just chasing daylight now," Limbaugh says.

Other than that, the two-hour trip is very quiet.

5:08 p.m. EST—The plane lands. This time, it's a small airport in southeastern Tennessee. Outside, the temperature is 61 degrees.

Limbaugh is greeted by a man whose father-in-law played at Alabama. Although this is Big Orange Country, Alabama has a shot at two prospects here.

5:17 p.m. CST—Limbaugh is back on the phone. On a small television, the evening news is on. The lead sports story might affect tonight's recruiting.

"Georgia is looking for a new athletic director and football coach," says the sportscaster. "Vince Dooley is stepping down ... ."

6:01 p.m. CST—This could be Mayberry. Or Anywhere USA On the main street, Christmas lights are seen in all directions.

Limbaugh has been looking forward to dinner. But the man in the car informs him that one of the recruit's mothers was fixing chili. Limbaugh rolls his eyes.

The car stops at Western Sizzler. Limbaugh orders coffee while his companion eats broiled chicken and baked potato.

The subject turns to eating. Surprisingly, it is an important part of recruiting.

Limbaugh tells a story about when he was at Ole Miss with Steve Sloan. They had two home visits scheduled, one at 5:30 p.m., the other at 7 p.m. The kids' mothers always fix dinner.

As usual, Sloan wouldn't eat.

"He would always say the same thing,' Limbaugh said. "That he had a stomach ailment. At the first house, the mother served cheeseburgers. Not just ordinary cheeseburgers, but huge ones."

Limbaugh wolfed them down. But Limbaugh abides by one golden rule of recruiting.

"If Mama's cooking, always ask for seconds."

In addition to the two huge burgers, he also had seconds on chocolate cake.

He felt like a stuffed pig.

But 90 minutes later, at another home, the dinner bell rang again.

Only this time it was deer chili and homemade pie á la mode. He had two servings of each.

During the recruiting season, Limbaugh gains about 25 pounds.

"Not this year," Limbaugh said.

"I'm not eating very much."

6:50 p.m. CST—Limbaugh wheels the car into a beautiful home nestled in the Tennessee woods. There is a satellite dish in the back. These people aren't millionaires. But compared to the other recruits today, they are living nicely.

"How you doin', you rascal?" Limbaugh says, shaking hands with the prospect at the door.

The prospect, a linebacker, is a tall kid. He is wearing a Coca-Cola shirt and jeans.

He is one of Tennessee's top 12 prospects. One service ranks him No. 48 in the South. He is not Everybody's All-American. Still, Alabama wants him.

The mother gets right to the heart of things.

"Would you like some deer chili [made of venison]?"

"Shoot yeah," says Limbaugh, smiling like a Cheshire cat.

Five minutes later, Limbaugh is eating a bowl of chili. He attacks it like one of those dogs on the Alpo commercials.

"This is really good," Limbaugh says. "You've got a gift here. I'm telling you. This is the best deer chili I've ever had," Limbaugh says, as if he would know.

After a few minutes, Limbaugh is at it again.

"Can I have a little more chili," Limbaugh tells the mother. "I tell you one thing, when Coach Curry comes to visit, you're going to have to give him some of this."

7:32 p.m. CST—There are posters decorating the walls of the prospect's bedroom. But the one directly over the player's bed is that of Bill Curry. To the side, there is one of Tennessee coach Johnny Majors.

"Hey, that Tennessee poster is just taking space," the prospect says.

When the parents and Limbaugh leave the room, the kid is asked about the decision.

"I'd like to take some other visits. Ole Miss wants me to take one. I'm going to see if Tennessee will offer me one even though I'm not sure I would take it."

He is also considering Vanderbilt, Georgia, and Georgia Tech.

"But I'm going to Alabama."

7:46 p.m. CST—Back in the den Limbaugh is having some more chili.

"I'm telling you, Coach Curry is going to have to eat some of this," Limbaugh tells the mother. "My one request when he comes: Deer chili. That's my one request."

One wonders if Limbaugh has something against Curry.

For the next five minutes, Limbaugh talks about the Alabama tradition.

"The worst thing that will happen to you at Alabama is you'll graduate," Limbaugh says.

"That's true," says the father, who looks more anxious about signing with Alabama than the kid.

8:19 p.m. CST—Back in the car for the 20-mile drive down the dark country road. There is one more recruit to see.

Oh, by the way, Limbaugh is asked: "How was the chili?" No answer.

8:42 p.m. CST—Limbaugh has found the house of the top recruit in the State of Tennessee.

It is a poor neighborhood, across the street from the railroad track. There is no satellite dish in this backyard.

As Limbaugh walks to the door, a train comes by, making a loud, thundering noise.

The player is alone. His mother died a few months ago. There is no sign of the father.

The house is decorated for Christmas. In the other room, a television set is on. Auburn is ahead of Vanderbilt. But it's only the first half.

"I was about to give up on you," says the player, a 6-4, 200-pound linebacker. "I was about to go to sleep."

Realizing the time, Limbaugh doesn't waste any.

"We're on the verge of some big things. It looks like we're about to have one of those national championship-type recruiting years."

The player shakes his head. But he also has a question.

"What happened to Coach (Chip) Wisdom?" he asks.

Wisdom, an Alabama assistant, resigned two weeks ago. He was asked to.

"It's no different than anything that happens on every staff in America," Limbaugh says.

Limbaugh asks the kid about his visits. Each kid is allowed five.

"Florida, Iowa, Alabama, UCLA, and LSU."

He says Tennessee is not out of the picture. As he finishes his answer the phone rings. It is cordless.

"Yeah, coach," the player says, somewhat bored.

The coach is from Ohio State.

A few minutes later, there is another call. This one from Arkansas.

The Arkansas coach asks about his basketball game the night before. This happens to every recruit. Coaches call all the time, just to tell the kid they are interested.

"That's the funniest coach I've ever talked to," says the kid, hanging up the phone.

Being funny doesn't matter in recruiting. He is still not going to Arkansas.

Limbaugh is back into *the pitch*.

"Alabama has won 11 national championships ... Alabama has been to more bowl games ... Been on television ... Alabama has won more SEC championships... . The worst thing that will happen to you at Alabama is you'll graduate."

Limbaugh leans closer.

"I want you wearing that Crimson jersey ... . we want to win a national championship while you're there. A couple of them. You're the kind of guy that can help us."

The kid has a nickname. Limbaugh tells him he'll talk to Curry about putting it on his jersey.

The player is impressed.

It is also getting late.

"What are you looking for that we don't have to offer?"

"I don't know."

"Between me and you, you want to come to Alabama, don't you?"

"I want to," says the kid, "but you know there are three or four schools I'm still looking at."

He mentions Florida again. Tennessee is mentioned.

"Something about that program just isn't right," says the kid, referring to Tennessee.

The kid tells Limbaugh it may take him awhile to decide.

"Where do I stand with you?" he asks.

"You have a scholarship until the last day of recruiting," Limbaugh says.

Only the best players are told that.

9:44 p.m. CST—Back to the airport.

"It's been a good day," Limbaugh says. "It's been a very good day."

10:17 p.m. CST—The plane takes off. Limbaugh is dog-tired. But there is no time for a nap. He takes out some cards and begins writing each of the four prospects he has just seen a short note. He will write the kids nearly every day. He'll also call them on the phone.

10:57 p.m. CST–Outside the window, the moon is shining bright. Up in the distance, the lights of Tuscaloosa can barely be seen. After the plane lands, Limbaugh gets into the car. He drives past another airport hangar and points to a car.

"That's Coach Curry's car. He must be visiting a prospect tonight."

11:17 p.m. CST—After 17 hours and 58 minutes, having traveled 2,100 miles, the day is finally over. The car pulls into Limbaugh's driveway.

The house lights are off.

"I'm looking forward to tomorrow," Limbaugh said. "I'm flying commercial so I don't have to leave until 7 a.m. That means I'll get to sleep late, probably 5:30."

On the car radio, the disk jockey gives the time and temperature. He plays a song. As Limbaugh closes his back door, Rod Stewart is singing "Forever Young."

One of my favorite columns and most interesting journeys. It was more fascinating since Curry and I were not speaking at the time. When I asked Limbaugh why Curry allowed me to go on this trip, he responded: "I don't know ... I never asked him."

MARCH 18, 1989

South Alabama responds to halftime challenge from Arrow

ATLANTA—As the South Alabama players gathered in their locker room at halftime yesterday, their faces were drawn. They trailed Alabama 49-33.

They had the look of losers.

And that's what many of the 12,349 fans in The Omni were calling the Sun Belt Conference champions.

Meanwhile, inside the South Alabama locker room, the joint was jumping. Blackboards were being smashed. There was ranting and raving.

Everything Coach Ronnie Arrow had worked so hard for was going down the drain. His team was playing as if it were in a fraternity league instead of the NCAA Tournament.

Perhaps that is one reason he unleashed a halftime talk that might rival Knute Rockne's "Win one for the Gipper" speech.

Usually, such chatter is private. Only players and managers hear the pep talk. But Arrow was screaming so loudly that an innocent bystander (blush!) was able to hear it through walls 30 feet away. Curiosity might have killed the cat. But not me.

Arrow told his players they weren't worth, among other things, horse manure. He used a few other slang words to describe his feelings. Most often, you hear such words in Marine barracks.

Then, he changed gears.

Now, he had their attention.

"You guys are winners," Arrow told his team. "You won the Sun Belt championship ... You won the tournament. ... It's a good league. ... The SEC can kiss my ass."

Arrow paused a moment, then continued.

"Can we win this game?"

Some noise was heard.

"Can we win this game?" he asked, louder.

His team made more noise.

"We are going to win this game!"

First thought: This guy is a nut. There is no way the Jaguars can come back from a 16-point deficit. They are playing Alabama, after all.

Well, so much for nuts.

Twenty minutes later, Arrow was being mobbed by his players, who were celebrating the biggest victory in South Alabama history.

It was an extraordinary comeback. And when Jeff Hodge hit a 3-pointer from 23 feet with four seconds remaining, giving the Jaguars an 86-84 victory over Alabama, it was hard not to shake one's head in disbelief.

Certainly, there will be questions raised about Alabama's collapse. Should senior forward Michael Ansley have been pulled late in the game with four fouls? There were others as well.

On the other side, it is hard not to notice in the box score that Alabama only shot 10 free throws, while South Alabama attempted 35.

The officiating was awful.

But the halftime talk by Arrow certainly wasn't.

"That's just Coach Arrow," Hodge said.

"If the team is not playing well, he is going to rant and rave. He woke us up. He knew we could play with anybody in the country because we have a good team.

"He got our attention. He told us the SEC isn't any better than our league. He told us we could play with anybody in the country."

Someone asked Arrow about the halftime chat. Pretty normal?

"I just asked them to please get out and play and they responded," Arrow said.

When told that his speech could be heard outside the locker room, he simply smiled.

A few feet away, Alabama coach Wimp Sanderson wasn't smiling. His worst fears had come true.

His Alabama team, a marvelous team that had come so far, now would go home losers. Sanderson probably could imagine UAB coach Gene Bartow back in Birmingham laughing his head off.

"I'm 51 years old and have to go on with my life," Sanderson said. "We worked so hard to get here. Basketball coaching is an up-and-down thing. You're on Cloud Nine sometimes. Sometimes, you're down in the dumps. Needless to say, right now, I'm down in the dumps."

While some people will consider South Alabama's victory an upset, interestingly, the Jaguars went off in Las Vegas as a 1½-point favorite, according to Danny Sheridan, who makes odds for *USA Today*.

When the NCAA pairings were announced on Sunday, the Tide was posted as a 3½-point favorite. However, the bettors put their money on South Alabama.

One of the all-time upsets. It also caused me problems because I told my radio audience if South Alabama beat Alabama, I would crawl to Mobile. I did make the trip and crawled across a patio in front of cameras and reporters. Of course, I got a free trip to Mobile, which is like getting a free trip to Cleveland.

APRIL 6, 1989

Augusta National all it's cracked up to be

AUGUSTA, Georgia—So this is Augusta. It couldn't be, I thought. All my life, I've read about this sleepy, Southern town on the Savannah River.

But as I drove down Washington Road for the first time yesterday, heading for you know where, I couldn't believe it.

Paul Harvey, the radio commentator, once said this was the sort of place where people went to the barber shop to watch haircuts.

Yet, I saw nothing quiet or quaint about it.

Along Washington Road, there are so many fast-food restaurants and gas stations, the mayor of Hoover would have felt right at home.

Still, the sign said, "Masters, straight ahead."

But all I could see was a Texaco station on the corner and a Domino's pizza parlor.

For days, I had dreamed about watching Jack Nicklaus and Greg Norman play the Amen Corner. Suddenly, all I could think about was a 12-inch cheese pizza with black olives. Thin and crispy, of course.

Finally, the sign came into focus. There was no neon flashing. It was simple, green and white with a splash of red.

"Augusta National Golf Club. Members Only."

Then, it began to hit me. As the clubhouse came in focus, springtime came alive in all its glory. The azaleas, those famous azaleas I had seen every April on CBS, were everywhere.

The place looked more like a nursery than a golf club.

As I looked around, my mind drifted for a moment. Suddenly, I thought of Mack Shoemaker, the veteran golf writer for the *Birmingham Post-Herald.*

The Masters was his favorite assignment. He lived for it. But on January 20, Mack died of cancer. He was buried wearing a Masters hat.

Now, the Masters assignment had fallen to me.

I've always wanted to come to Augusta—just once—to experience these hallowed grounds. To see and be seen.

Yet, somehow, I would rather have been in Tuscaloosa yesterday covering Bobby Humphrey and Gene Jelks while reading Mack Shoemaker's byline from Augusta.

Mack always used to say this place was golf's answer to heaven. And walking around the plush grounds, finally, I saw his point.

Inside the gates, it was a different world. Today, the golfers get down to serious business.

But yesterday was fun day at Augusta. Most of the golfers play practice rounds in the morning because the afternoon is reserved for the Par-3 tournament.

It makes little sense. But like everything here at Augusta, it is a tradition.

Most of the action here yesterday was not on the course, but around the great water oak tree on the veranda, just outside the famed clubhouse.

This is where the elite meet, eat, and greet.

In Los Angeles, you used to be able to go to Schwaab's to find a rising star. At Augusta, it is the oak tree.

It doesn't take long to find the biggest star in the golfing galaxy.

Arnold Palmer has arrived.

"How you doing ... Jack," Palmer says, as he reads the man's first name off a badge.

"Great, Arnie. Do you mind if we take a picture?"

Sure, Palmer minds. But he doesn't say that. Instead, like he does a thousand times a week, Palmer smiles.

Interestingly, Palmer is in no hurry to practice. And you really can't blame him. What good would it do him?

Golf has made Palmer a millionare. But the 59-year-old golfer hasn't won a regular PGA tour event since the 1973 Bob Hope. His last victory at the Masters was in 1964.

Still, he shows up at all the big tournaments. Without fail, he is humiliated.

A few minutes later, someone spots Paul Hornung, the former star of the Green Bay Packers. Hornung isn't drawing flies.

Neither is Chris Schenkel, who used to be ABC's top golf announcer. These days, he hangs out on Saturdays at bowling lanes, describing strikes and spares.

Dan Jenkins, who used to be *Sports Illustrated*'s golf writer, is gabbing with Alex Hawkins, the former football star. Both are talking about recent books they have written.

Nobody is listening.

Inside the clubhouse, a familiar face is spotted. Hall Thompson, the man who built Shoal Creek, is having a quiet lunch. Thompson, of course, is a member at Augusta.

Outside on the veranda, Charley Boswell and his wife are also lunching.

"I've been coming here for 30 years," sayd the world's best-known blind golfer.

As always, Boswell greets a visitor, saying, "Good to see you."

A few feet from Boswell, Jim Nantz has drawn the biggest crowd since Palmer left 30 minutes earlier.

Nantz has replaced Brent Musburger this year as host of the tournament for CBS.

It might be April in Augusta, but Nantz is still running on March Madness standard time.

After the NCAA final in Seattle on Monday night, he flew all night to Augusta. The bags under his eyes are his confirmation.

Someone asks whether Steve Fischer will get the Michigan job. But Nantz doen't answer.

For Nantz and everyone else here, that was yesterday's news.

Today, the Masters begins. And nothing else seems to matter.

To say I was excited about my first trip to Augusta would be an understatement. It probably is my favorite sporting event, that is, other than the Auburn-Alabama game and annual monster tractor pull every spring at the Birmingham Civic Center.

APRIL 10, 1989

Hoch blows his shot at immortality

AUGUSTA—The green jacket is the most coveted garment in the world of sports. To own one is to be part of a special royalty only a handful of men—such as Palmer, Player, and Nicklaus—has experienced.

And early last night, as darkness clouded the beauty of this pastoral garden known as Augusta National, Scott Hoch stood a mere 24 inches from immortality.

Only two feet. All he had to do was make the white ball disappear.

He had failed earlier at No. 17, so now, the 33-year-old Floridian was in a sudden-death playoff with Nick Faldo.

The Masters championship went to the survivor.

Almost everyone figured it would be Hoch. Faldo had bogeyed the hole. In his native England, the headline writers probably already had put in type: "Nick Foldo Flops Again."

So Hoch took his time. He walked around the 10th green looking over the putt. In the background, the spectators watched. Stillness. No one breathed.

The only sound that could be heard was raindrops, splattering the green velvet fairways of Augusta.

Finally, Hoch moved closer to the ball.

The putter moved back. There was contact. For a moment, the ball seemed suspended on the ground before it moved.

In unison, the gallery sighed. Hoch's eyes bulged and his body shaked, almost as if he had been hooked up to an electric chair and the switch pulled.

He missed. And no one could believe it.

For those of you who don't follow golf closely, two-foot putts usually are automatic. On Sunday afternoons at the club, they often are called "gimmes."

But in a sudden-death playoff at the Masters, there is no such thing.

And probably there never will be such a thing as a green jacket in Scott Hoch's locker at Augusta.

"I'm glad I don't carry a gun," the Wake Forest graduate said later at what best could be described as, well, a wake.

Everyone knew it was over then. And on the next hole, it was, when Faldo sank a 25-foot putt to capture golf's most prestigious prize.

For Hoch, there was no shelter from the storm.

"It's frustrating," Hoch admitted. "I'm very disappointed."

Perhaps Hoch was nervous. After all, millions of people throughout the world were watching on television.

The man had not won a tournament since 1984, when he won the Quad Cities Open. Actually, his greatest claim to fame is to have played on the same golf team at Wake Forest with Curtis Strange.

And, of course, you Saturday afternoon television watchers probably know his brother, Buddy, who is a professional bowler.

Buddy was unavailable for comment afterward. But one could bet he would have described Hoch's two-foot miss as "a gutter ball."

So, again: Was Hoch nervous?

"I wasn't," said Hoch, whose 69-74-71-69-283 finish still earned him $100,000.

"I just had the putter lined up wrong. I guess I picked a bad time for that."

In all fairness, Hoch wasn't the only golfer who fell only a putt short.

In one of the most dramatic days in the storied history of Augusta National, one by one, the giants of the game fell victim to the course.

At times, it seemed there were more leaders on the scoreboard than suitors for Eastern Airlines.

Ben Crenshaw and Greg Norman missed the playoff by bogeying the final hole. Seve Ballesteros also stumbled on the back nine, missing the playoff by two shots.

For Norman, it was a familiar feeling. In 1987, he lost a playoff to Larry Mize when the Georgian sank a chip shot. Last year, he fired a stunning 64 on the final day, only to finish fourth.

And yesterday, he shot a 67. Again, Norman was barely short.

As he walked into the locker room following his round, Norman threw up his hands and said: "What do I have to do to win this son of a ... ?"

Until yesterday, Scott Hoch wouldn't have understood the feeling that Norman was now experiencing.

Norman is known throughout the world.

Hoch probably is known only in Davenport, Iowa, the site of his last victory.

"I could not believe it," Hoch said, still talking about the putt.

Outside, the spectators who had pulled so hard for him only a few minutes earlier, no longer were interested.

As they marched out of Augusta National to the sound of falling raindrops, Hoch was left alone in his misery.

"I had been making those putts all week," Hoch said, trying to convince himself and the media.

But the media no longer was interested in him. Nick Faldo had arrived.

And he was wearing the green jacket.

To this day, Hoch's missed putt remains one of the heart-wrenching memories of my sporting career. Of course, I have recreated that putt many times since on the golf course.

August 16, 1989

Is Curry next on the firing line?

Now that athletic director Steve Sloan has been swept out the door, the question some Alabama fans are asking is appropriate: Will football coach Bill Curry be next?

Certainly, the firing of Sloan yesterday will not make living easy for Curry, who now has lost his two chief supporters in Sloan and former university president Joab Thomas.

But one thing seems clear.

If Roger Sayers, the new president at Alabama, can lower the boom on Sloan—an Alabama man to the core—it's doubtful he'll feel any pain if he has to fire the coach from Georgia Tech.

Certainly, that will be the speculation in the wake of this bizarre bombshell.

But did Sloan deserve to be fired?

Sure, he made mistakes as athletic director. But perhaps his biggest mistake was his inability to project himself as a more powerful figure.

Instead of being forceful like his rival at Auburn, Sloan, who is a genuinely nice man, often came off as a buffoon.

When you asked someone for an opinion on Auburn athletic director and head football coach Pat Dye, you heard words like tough and feared. About Sloan, a typical response was he could hit a great 3-iron in the wind.

When Sloan made a hole-in-one during a Southeastern Conference golf outing in Destin, Florida, last June (his third in his lifetime), one Alabama man was not impressed.

"I'm sick and tired of hearing what a great golfer Sloan is," the man said. "If he spent less time on the golf course, our athletic department might not be in such a mess."

Aside from his golfing reputation, Sloan often was criticized for his handling of the Iron Bowl site dispute. Alabama fans often have said if Ray Perkins or Bear Bryant were still around, the Tide would not be going to Auburn. The reality is that Bryant couldn't have done any better than Sloan, but the perception was different.

Another question raised in all of this is whether or not Curry's position is stronger with the demise of Sloan. And whether or not Curry's fingerprints are on the murder weapon.

Since the two men arrived together in January 1987, the general perception has been that they were close friends.

But were they really?

Sloan has been handcuffed by the fact he was Curry's boss, but had no hand in hiring him. Some people believe he showed weakness by accepting the job without some role in hiring the football coach.

The most public division between Curry and Sloan was over the decision last fall not to send Alabama to College Station, Texas, to play Texas A&M because of hurricane warnings.

Sloan made the decision to go. But Curry said he wasn't taking the team. Sloan backed down. Although it might have been the right decision, he looked like a wimp in the process.

Sloan took a brutal beating in the news media. At the same time, Curry was heralded by Alabama fans as a hero who cared more about saving lives than winning football games.

Lately, reports of friction over other athletic department matters have surfaced. One tale making the rounds was that Curry was trying to push Sloan out and become athletic director.

Last week, I asked Sloan about this. Sloan confirmed that he and Curry had a disagreement over something, but declined to be specific.

Four days later, Sloan was in Sayers's office, getting fired.

Although the timing was hard to figure, the dismissal really is not.

Last summer, these rumors were fast and furious that Sloan was going to be ousted and replaced by Lee Roy Jordan, the former Alabama linebacker.

Some people believed the publication of the story (in this space) actually might have helped Sloan keep his job because of backlash against Jordan.

Now that an opening has been created, will Sayers talk to Jordan? There seems to be little change.

Sayers said yesterday that the person chosen must have at least five years of experience in a senior administrative post in a successful Division I athletic program, a reputation "of impeccable integrity among the NCAA and other college athletic governing bodies, and a demonstrated record of commitment to high academic standards for student athletes."

The most prominent name heard is Hootie Ingram, the former Alabama man, who has done a splendid job in running the Florida State program. Ingram would be a popular choice among Alabama fans. Of course, if Ingram is hired, there would be immediate speculation about Florida State coach Bobby Bowden, whom many people believe should have gotten the job instead of Curry in the first place.

Of course, trying to figure out the next move in Tuscaloosa is extremely difficult. Seemingly the only thing known for sure is that Sloan is out and Sayers clearly is in charge of the school.

As for Curry, the questions will continue to be asked. And although Sayers denied any correlation between Sloan's firing and Curry's future, nothing seems certain anymore in Tuscaloosa.

Nothing, that is, except chaos.

Bill Curry blasted me after writing this column, saying it was terribly unfair. Of course, that is the singular reason I have chosen to recreate it in this book so he can have a lasting record of it.

OCTOBER 18, 1989

Majors confrontation makes trip worthwhile

KNOXVILLE— It had been a postcard perfect autumn day at the foot of the Smoky Mountains. But now, as dusk fell, the sky had been invaded by patches of black, while on the western horizon, angry storm clouds moved in.

Yet, inside the new athletic facility at the University of Tennessee, there was a feeling of calm and confidence as the school prepared for its biggest football game in 16 years.

And at the office of Tennessee football coach Johnny Majors, things were also quiet as I sat waiting for an appointment.

"Good afternoon, Big Orange Country," a secretary said.

The sound of that made me uncomfortable, although it shouldn't have.

After all, I was born and bred in Tennessee. My diploma is from here.

However, I was swallowing hard. I had the feeling one experiences as they wait for the doctor to call back with the results of the biopsy.

"Hello, Paul," Majors said, showing that famed toothy grin that sits in the middle of those ruddy cheeks.

"How are you doin'?"

Not bad, I thought to myself. Not bad at all. I've been in Knoxville 18 hours and not a single person had pulled a gun or taken a swing. So far, so good.

Perhaps this might be a good time to explain what I was doing here in the first place.

The Knoxville Quarterback Club had invited me to be guest speaker at its weekly luncheon. When I accepted the invitation last summer, the conventional wisdom was that I would preview the Alabama-Tennessee game. Perhaps I would even reminisce about my days in college.

But a certain column I wrote three weeks ago changed that.

After Majors blasted Auburn coach Pat Dye before the two teams met, saying, "he must be on good terms with the registrar," I struck back. I wrote a column saying Majors should take a good look in the mirror before casting stones at others.

I added: "That's assuming the mirror is still there and hasn't been stolen by one of Tennessee's football players."

I also mentioned a long list of Tennessee players who have encountered trouble with the law, even suggesting the school might change its name from "Rocky Top" to "Jailhouse Rock."

In the aftermath, there were some ugly things written and said about me in Knoxville. Radio stations conducted "Hate Paul Finebaum" contests. (They were very popular, by the way).

Someone went to the trouble of making several thousand copies of the column and distributing them in the Knoxville area.

So I was a little apprehensive as I stepped to the podium.

Most people were cordial at the meeting, although I did have someone sample my lunch before I ate it, just to be on the safe side.

One man, who proudly said, "I played for the General (as in Neyland)," asked me:

"Have you ever worn a jock strap at Neyland Stadium?"

I thought for a moment and responded: "No, I couldn't find one to fit."

The crowd softened up after that.

Feeling brave after the speech, I attempted to set up a meeting with Majors. I seriously doubted I'd get an appointment, but Majors's secretary said he could see me at 4:45 p.m.

So there I was.

At first, it was tense. I broached the subject first about the recent column. He listened intently. He told me to forget it, no hard feelings.

Deep down, I got the impression Majors was not mad, partly because he might have used the column to help fire up his team for Auburn.

We talked about running back Reggie Cobb and the flap over his drug-related expulsion from the team.

"A lot of people are now praising you for the stand you took?" I asked him.

"I wish I didn't have to be praised," Majors said. "I don't feel like popping my buttons off. I don't feel it's a great thing that happened.

It's just something that had to be done and the team comes first."

Majors impressed me during our meeting. I saw a different side of him, a more human side than I previously had seen.

Perhaps living through the nightmare of 1988, when his team lost six games, had affected him in a positive way. I was beginning to enjoy the conversation. I think he was, too.

But a glance at the clock told me time was short. Majors was due at practice in five minutes. I had a plane to catch in 45 minutes.

I stood up to leave, shaking his hand.

As I opened the office door, Majors called after me.

It startled me at first. What did he want? Was he going to take it all back? Or would he ask me for some information, such as whether or not Jeff Dunn would get any playing time at quarterback?

Actually, he wanted neither.

Johnny Majors simply looked at me and smiled. And then he said softly, "I hope you'll come back and see us."

I still can't believe I wasted an afternoon of my life meeting with John Majors. I must have been desperate for material or drunk or both.

DECEMBER 4, 1989

10-1 looks good, but the bottom line for Curry reads 0-10

AUBURN—The location was different. But some things never change.

On this historic Saturday, just "staying focused" couldn't win the biggest game of the year. Neither could shielding your players from the news media or threatening to cut off interviews if the questions concerned something other than *the game.*

The difference was recruiting and coaching, the key ingredients to a dominating football program. And for the past three years, Auburn coach Pat Dye has had the goods in those departments over Alabama coach Bill Curry.

But maybe preparation also played a part in Auburn's 30-20 victory over Alabama. Perhaps Dye's healthy approach of "having fun, this is not the end of the world," was better than Curry's tense, uptight, "boys let's treat this like Armageddon."

Some wonder if Curry's steely-eyed attitude might have been rubbed off on his players, because the Crimson Tide ended a brilliant regular season by saving its worst for last.

Instead of being loose and enjoying the moment for what it was, the Tide played as if it carried the world on its shoulders, straining and struggling to exorcise demons from within.

It was disappointing to watch because this team is capable of so much more than it showed. And to fall when it mattered most—with an undefeated season and a clear shot at the national championship on the line—only makes the hurt that much worse.

This is not to say Alabama hasn't had a good season. Only one other team—Colorado—was undefeated going into the first Saturday in December. But to some Alabama fans, going 10-1 and receiving a bid to the Sugar Bowl doesn't amount to a hill of beans.

The bottom line is beating Auburn.

Often in his speeches around the state, Curry says you ultimately have to be judged by your record—what is on the scoreboard at the end of the game.

In this case, the numbers he carries around his neck like a scarlet letter are 0-10—his record against Auburn. In some ways, that is unfair, considering seven of those losses were at Georgia Tech.

At Alabama, his record against Auburn is 0-3.

The last Alabama coach to go 0-3 against Auburn was J. B. "Ears" Whitworth.

As one prominent Alabama alum said Saturday while leaving the stadium, "Perkins, Bowden, and Schnellenberger would have never lost three in a row to Auburn with this talent."

Another one quickly chimed in, "Yeah, what happens when they pick up Georgia and Florida next year and Perkins's players are gone?"

Despite a 10-1 regular season, these questions linger in the back of the minds of many Alabama fans.

Another question being discussed is whether or not Curry will receive a contract extension. He is completing the third year of a five-year contract.

Curry was asked after the game if university officials have discussed the matter with him.

"No," Curry said. "I don't think that's for me to comment on. That's for the authorities and our administration to talk about anything like that. That's not for me to speak about publicly."

But two weeks ago, while addressing the Birmingham Rotary Club, Curry said recruits have asked for clarification about his future.

"That's the thing they asked last year, that's the thing they asked the year before and that's the thing they are going to continue to ask until there is total stability," Curry said.

But Alabama athletic director Hootie Ingram feels differently.

"This is just not the time to talk about it," Ingram said. "We have more important things to do.

Meanwhile, all is happy on the Plains.

Last month, some Auburn fans surprisingly were down on Dye. But with dominating victories over Georgia and Alabama, once again, Dye has proved his critics wrong and accomplished the job he was hired to do: Beat Alabama and, as a lesser priority, win the Southeastern Conference championship.

If anybody deserves a contract extension—as in lifetime—it is Dye.

Winning at least a share of three consecutive SEC titles puts him in the company of such distinguished coaches as Vince

Dooley, Bob Neyland, and the legendary Paul "Bear" Bryant. Because of that, coupled with four consecutive victories over Alabama, Dye is approaching legendary status in these parts.

As for Alabama, it has been a good season. A victory over Miami in the Sugar Bowl will cap Alabama's best season since Bryant.

But for many people, it will not be enough.

Beating Auburn is the bottom line. Beating Auburn determines whether you are successful.

"I accept the blame for this loss," Curry said. "It starts at the top and that's me. Now, it's another 365 days before we get an opportunity to redeem ourselves. That's a long, long time."

This loss effectively finished Curry at Alabama. And as they say down New Orleans way, "Laissez les bons temps rouler."

JANUARY 6, 1990

Once again, the perception's unfair

In the 1960s, the nation watched with horror as television and newspapers featured pictures from Alabama of police using firehoses and dogs on blacks.

While the nation might have held the state in contempt for its perceived racial policies, it looked differently on the University of Alabama football program and to its legendary coach, Paul "Bear" Bryant.

Today, nearly 30 years later, the perceptions of the state of Alabama and the football program now are the antithesis of what they used to be.

While many people have praised the state for making positive steps forward, pointing to Birmingham's black mayor and other achievements, many people in the nation now are sneering at the Alabama football program.

It all has stemmed from a perception that people in Alabama have treated Bill Curry unfairly.

By the time the stories about Alabama football have made it to California and New York—and parts in between—the national news media will have you believe that brick-throwing here is as popular as golf, hunting, and fishing.

Mark Bradley, an *Atlanta Constitution* sports columnist—who formerly worked in Lexington, Kentucky, and is a close friend of Bill Curry—began an article two day ago like this:

"It's said that a man ultimately winds up with the face he deserves. Here's hoping that the imbecile segments of Alabama fans will get the football coach it warrants—an Alabama homeboy to come into Tuscaloosa and make a dishonorable mess of the program and still lose to Auburn every year. How sweet that'd be.

"How sweet that it seems the imbeciles won't have Bill Curry to kick around anymore."

Bradley's article was not the only one of its kind.

A column by Paul Daugherty of the *Cincinnati Post* went a step further. He writes about a guy bellied up to bar in New Orleans, who has been a follower of the Tide for 32 years, talking about the perception of Alabama football fans.

Wrote Daugherty:

"Fair or not, Crimson Tide football has done much to perpetuate the notion there are more yahoos per square mile in Alabama than anywhere else on Earth. How else do you explain a group of fans who have treated shabbily a coach who led their team to a 10-2 record?"

I am not naive enough to say Bill Curry was greeted with open arms upon his arrival three years ago.

But should he have been?

Alabama fans preferred a proven coach such as Bobby Bowden, Howard Schnellenberger, or Danny Ford.

Instead, they got Curry, who showed up with mediocre credentials (31-43-4 coaching record) from an even more suspect football school (Georgia Tech). Let it be said there were no pep rallies at Tech begging him to stay.

Crimson Tide fans didn't feel the selection process was anything more than a railroad job by Joab Thomas, then Alabama's president.

To Curry's credit, he won over many people with polished speaking skills, which he probably honed as a sportscaster in Atlanta.

Curry told Alabama fans he had to earn their respect.

"The great thing about football is that you don't do it with your mouth or in the newspaper," Curry said. "You do it between the white lines. We promise to give you what you're used to at Alabama."

But he didn't.

In his first season, Curry went 7-5 with an unforgettable loss to Memphis State.

"This will not happen again," Curry assured Alabama fans. "We will not tolerate it."

But 51 weeks later, Alabama lost to an inferior Ole Miss team at homecoming.

Not only was his team unable to beat Auburn for the second consecutive year, there were numerous discipline problems—a sharp contrast to the Bryant and Perkins eras. And last spring, there were shocking revelations on the academic front. A strong academic program inherited from Perkins was in shambles.

This season, to Curry's credit, he finally was able to turn the program around and earn the support he deserved.

As Alabama marched toward the Sugar Bowl, hardly a naysayer was heard. Instead, there was an outpouring of affection and enthusiasm not seen in Tuscaloosa in more than a decade.

In Baton Rouge, Louisiana, following a victory over LSU, the fans chanted long into the night; "We love Bill ... We love Bill."

It was one of the most emotional outbursts of affection this writer has witnessed in many years of covering college football.

Even though Curry lost to Auburn for the third consecutive year (at Auburn), there were few negative comments heard.

And nearly 40,000 fans flocked to New Orleans to cheer the Tide on against Miami in the Sugar Bowl. Plus, a three-year contract extension was offered a week after the Auburn loss.

So the question now remains: Were Alabama fans treating Bill Curry shabbily?

No, they weren't.

And it disappoints me when the national media creates the perception that everyone in Alabama is a rube who heads to the hardware store to buy bricks anytime Alabama trails at halftime.

This is a great state, and most people in it are very sensible—even when it comes to Alabama football.

We are not a bunch of imbeciles and rednecks. In Alabama, there are doctors, lawyers, factory workers, and farmers—all genuine, decent, hardworking citizens.

It probably would surprise people in Atlanta, New York, and Los Angeles that we also get cable television in Alabama, read *The Wall Street Journal,* and drive BMWs as well as pickup trucks.

Yes, one person threw a brick through Curry's office window. And we've heard Curry say one person called in a death threat.

Gerry Faust was harassed during his five years at Notre Dame. But much to Faust's credit, he bit the bullet and worked to the end, never blaming his problems on others. And today, he still doesn't.

One person sent a moving van to Bill Battle's home in Knoxville. Did the state of Tennessee get a black eye as a result?

However, because of a single brick tossed through an office window—coupled with a coach continually crying about not being accepted out of one side of his mouth while saying he's not concerned about the critics out of the other—the school's football program has been tainted.

So whose fault is it that the University of Alabama, a school with a rich and storied football tradition, now has a temporary black eye?

Is it the fans' or alumni's fault?

Or is it someone else's?

I have always felt Bill Curry—even while he was coach—tried to delineate Alabama football fans as rubes and rednecks, who spend their days munching moon pies and slurping RC Cola. I wonder where he ever got that idea.

Portrait of the columnist as a young troublemaker: Finebaum, senior year of high school, 1972.

From October, 1977. Finebaum working at the school newspaper. Yep, he once had hair.

A group of sportswriters with Coach Bryant on December 15, 1982. Later that night, Bryant coached his last game in the Liberty Bowl in Memphis. Finebaum was the one with the beard.

September, 1984. Even lovable Big Al had strong feelings about Finebaum.

Paul Finebaum, with a County Agent in 1984, milking a cow after losing a bet that Auburn would finish No. 1 in at least one poll.

Above A 1987 photo shows Finebaum in a rare moment with Alabama coach Bill Curry. You could sense how happy he was to be playing golf with Curry.

Left Another lost bet from April, 1989. Finebaum said he would crawl to Mobile if South Alabama beat Alabama in the NCAA tournament.

Left Another lost bet for Finebaum. This one, in April, 1990, at Auburn's A-Day, had the sports columnist riding a tractor. He had said if Auburn beat Alabama in 1989, he would ride a tractor to Auburn.

Below Pat Dye coaches Finebaum to victory in his 1990 tractor ride from Birmingham to Auburn.

WRIGHT CONCERT HALL
SAMFORD UNIVERSITY
TUESDAY, APRIL 23, 1991
7:00 P.M.

TICKETS
$10

In support of Vestavia Hills Schools' Programs for Academic Excellence

ROASTERS INCLUDE:

M.C. : John Ed Willoughby

Pat Dye

Ray Perkins

Tim Brando (ESPN)

Danny Sheridan (CNN/USA Today)

& others scheduled to appear!

Tickets available at Vestavia Hills schools and at the door.

Poster from the Finebaum Roast in 1991.

April, 1991. Finebaum roast. From left: Wimp Sanderson, Pat Dye, Finebaum, Ray Perkins, Tim Brando, Danny Sheridan, and John Ed Willoughby.

Tommy Charles with a bag over his head at the Finebaum roast. It definitely improved his appearance.

Above Sign from Frat Row in Auburn in November, 1993.

Left Banner hanging at Alabama-South Carolina game in October, 1993 displaying frustration by South Carolina fans after a stinging Finebaum column.

August, 1993. Finebaum and Chi Chi.

August, 1993. Finebaum shares a laugh with Ronnie Bruno, Gene Hallman, and Dr. Jim Andrews.

Left August, 1993. Finebaum and Charles Barkley at the Bruno's Memorial Classic.

Below June, 1994. Bruno's Memorial Classic Pro-Am. Left to right: HealthSouth Chairman Richard Scrushy, Charlie Chase of The Nashville Network, PGA pro Bob Murphy, Finebaum, and Mr. Potatoe Head himself, former Vice-President Dan Quayle.

Above Finebaum interviews Gene Stallings during the 1994 Bruno's Memorial Classic.

Left Finebaum (in a rare good mood) on the WERC set during the 1994 Bruno's Memorial Classic.

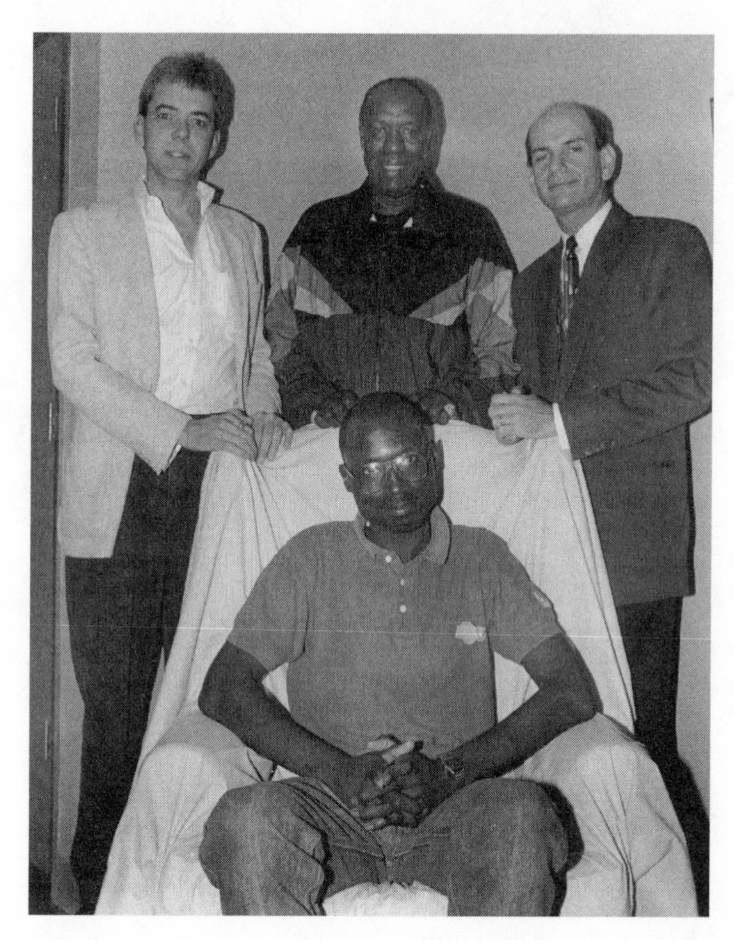

Finebaum, with talk show hosts Tim Lennox and Shelly Stewart, at the home of Don from Downtown.

May 12, 1990

Will more sex get jocks past first base, or not?

As Andy Rooney likes to say, "Have you wondered why athletes look so uptight when the ball game is on the line?"

"Have you ever wondered why they are always spitting and clutching themselves? Have you ever wondered why they are always hugging one another after home runs and patting each other on the fanny?"

Well, this week, we might have finally unlocked the door to Pandora's Box.

And we did all this without the help of Dr. Ruth.

The debate has nothing to do with the relationship between sneakers and gang violence or whether or not white basketball players can jump higher than blacks.

Folks, we're talking S-E-X here. You may have heard of it.

The superpower debate began a few days ago when Azeglio Vicini, coach of the Italian national soccer team, instructed his players not to engage in sex until the World Cup tournament in Italy ends July 8.

This weekend will be the last at liberty for the players before a long period of "seclusion," Vicini said, and added: "Chastity of players prior to and during a major competition has been a long-debated but unsolved problem."

It not only affects soccer. It has touched baseball, among others.

Former baseball manager Casey Stengel once said:

"I don't mind players having sex before games. It's what they have to go through to get it that bothers me."

It also used to worry Bear Bryant.

On the subject of Kenny Stabler, Bryant once mumbled: "I don't want him leaving his best stuff in the parking lot the night before a game."

Joe Namath was famous for coming home in the wee hours of the morning just in time to shave and get out to Shea Stadium and throw the winning score.

Boxing has probably drawn the most discussion over the years.

Muhammad Ali used to abstain from sex for six weeks prior to a fight. He said it made him mean and angry.

Following a loss to Buster Douglas, former champ Mike Tyson blamed his downfall on pretty women.

"Before (losing), you know, I had a great deal, I mean a big voracious appetite with the women and stuff," Tyson said.

Perhaps Tyson should go back to training his old way. Instead of having sex with women, he used to just throw them out of windows, along with the furniture.

Obviously, the Denver Broncos must spend a lot of time with their wives before Super Bowl appearances.

On the other hand, San Francisco is reputed to be the most sexually open city in the nation. But the Bay Area had the two participants in the World Series and the Super Bowl champs.

Dr. Ray Brown, who is affiliated with the Alabama Sports Medicine Clinic at the HealthSouth Medical Center, doesn't believe there is a direct correlation between celibacy and athletic performance.

"There just isn't anything to it," Brown said. "In fact, there are those who believe sex is one of the best ways of relieving tension before a big game."

Brown also points to a study, published in the March issue of the *The Physician and Sports Medicine*, that backs up that claim.

"Given the fact that intercourse is relatively undemanding physically, it's difficult to see how the idea of abstinence as a beneficial training regimen ever became so entrenched," the report said.

The article mentions a story about Dave Wottle, who won the 800-meter run in the 1972 Olympic Summer Games, who said he had sex shortly before the event.

There have even been reports of sex in the middle of an event.

One story going around is that during a race in New York, one male marathoner and a female left midway through and went back to her hotel. They had sex, and he rejoined the marathon.

Dr. Ron Stainback, a clinical psychologist at UAB, is another who takes exception to the notion.

"That really is kind of fallacious thinking," Stainback said. "There is really no indication of that. Now, certainly you don't want to pull something all night ... but within reason, I would not think sex is disruptive to athletic performance."

Regardless, this has certainly spurred on an interesting debate. From a personal standpoint, I'm just glad it has been confined to sports. With my luck, a new report will come out this fall stating that sports columnists are less creative following sex.

If that happens, can you imagine the orders I'll get from my boss in the weeks preceding the Alabama-Auburn game?

My only regret about this article was that I didn't have enough time to thoroughly research it.

JUNE 18,1990

He drank; now bars close on him

Tom Cox has a lot of time these days to think about what might have been. Yesterday marked his third consecutive Father's Day behind bars.

Memories are painful late at night, especially those of his teenage daughter he no longer knows.

Memories of his golf career are as distant as the Milky Way.

Twenty years ago, he was the finest junior golfer in the state. Who knows? If things had worked out differently, he might have been at Medinah yesterday playing in the U.S. Open instead of sitting in a stinking 8-foot by 12-foot prison cell at the West Jefferson Correctional Facility.

"Had he directed all of his energies, there is just no telling where he could have gone," said Mike Griffin, an old friend who now is Auburn's golf coach.

"He was one of the best to ever come out of the state."

From Enterprise, Cox went to Auburn, where he served as team captain in 1971.

Although he was a fine golfer, Cox never reached his potential. So he chose law school instead of PGA Tour school.

Cox graduated from Cumberland Law School in 1974 and went to work for Bill Baxley in the state attorney general's office.

Along the way, Cox married a beauty queen, who happened to be the niece of a former Alabama governor. They had a baby girl.

Cox was living the All-American life. But there was a deep, dark secret, one that soon became all too well known.

He was an alcoholic.

His marriage fell apart. He lost several jobs. It wasn't long before money ran through his hands like sand in an hourglass.

When friends quit lending him money, he turned to writing bogus checks.

All to pay for booze.

One morning, he had the shakes but no money. He ended up pawning an $800 set of golf clubs for a bottle of bourbon.

"I'm laughing," Cox said as he told the story. "But inside, I am crying."

Other than the white uniform on his back with the number 131853, Cox doesn't look much different than a thousand other guys in their early forties.

But his life is very different.

Instead of sharing a house with his former beauty queen wife, he shares an 8-by-12 cell with another felon.

Instead of a white picket fence around his home, there is one made of barbed wire. There are guard towers and guns.

I am the first visitor Cox has had since arriving at this prison five months ago.

Cox had written me a letter with a simple request. He wanted me to let his 89-year-old aunt in Enterprise know where a copy of a preseason football magazine could be purchased.

But after checking into his background, I went to visit him as well as to deliver the magazine.

He told his life story. Much of it involved drinking.

"It's ruined three marriages," Cox said.

"My last wife quit me and married a truck driver."

How did it begin?

"I guess at Auburn," Cox said. "We'd have beer every Friday or Saturday night for a quarter. But that was all."

The drinking began to intensify when he worked in Montgomery for the attorney general's office. He later took a job for a law firm in Birmingham. His main responsibility was as a lobbyist in Montgomery.

"I got a lot done there," Cox said. "I just burned up the legislature that year."

Cox also burned up the bars.

"Of course, being a lobbyist is a drinking job," Cox said. "I was perfect for it, sitting around with legislators all night."

Eventually, the legislators had to leave the bars to go back to work or home. But Cox stayed behind. He never missed the last call of the night.

Finally, he moved to Florida, taking a job as a general counsel for a title company.

As fast as he could run, he couldn't outrun the law.

He was in and out of jail, never spending more than a night or two, usually on a DUI charge.

But his hard luck turned worse a few years back.

While visiting family in Alabama, he was charged with theft of property for writing a bad $150 check. Another charge was forging a $15 check.

He pleaded guilty to both and received a three-year sentence. He went to jail, and things went from bad to worse.

Cox failed to return one night while out on an eight-hour pass. He was sentenced to three more years (to run concurrently).

In the eyes of the Department of Corrections, he was a security risk. So five months ago, he was sent to West Jefferson, the most maximum-secure prison in the Alabama system.

When you ask him to explain the past, Cox has difficulty.

"So much of it is a fog," Cox said. "I just can't remember the years between 1984 and 1987."

That was then. Now, all he wants is a chance.

Cox is due to be released in September, but there might be more warrants out there upon his release.

"There is a long list of people he owes money," Griffin said. "And that includes me."

Cox understands how his former friends feel.

"Everybody kind of turns against you when you go to prison," Cox said. "But I hope people will give me a chance. I know my record is not good. It may be 25 pages long, but it's nothing but DUIs and checks. There is no violence. I've never even been in a good fist fight."

Outside the office where Cox is sitting, there are prisoners in the yard. They are shoveling dirt in 94-degree heat as the sun blazes down on them.

Inside, Tom Cox finished his story. Though painful, it has proved to be a catharsis for him.

"I have lost a beautiful family," Cox said. "I have paid my time. All I need is a chance. It's just not right to keep me here any longer. You just can't keep a man in prison forever."

And then he was gone. Back to cell block 2-83, back to a life behind bars.

Tom Cox called me the day he got out of prison. But I never called him back. I'm sure he wanted money. But I have often wondered what happened to him.

AUGUST 4, 1990

Do they serve crow in Ventura, Woody?

Among the many thousands of words written across the globe in the past few weeks about Shoal Creek, perhaps the most ridiculous came from Woody Woodburn, a sports columnist from the *Star-Free Press* in Ventura, Calif.

Woodburn's two columns on Shoal Creek were picked up by the Scripps Howard News Service and published in the *Birmingham Post-Herald*.

Much of what I'd like to say to Mr. Woodburn is not printable in a family newpaper. What I can say follows in a missive I have forwarded to Mr. Woodburn.

Mr. Woody Woodburn
Ventura Star-Free Press
Ventura, Calif.

Dear Mr. Woodburn:

I feel certain the past four days have not been pleasant, knowing that we bigots and racists here in Alabama were able to straighten out the Shoal Creek problem without bloodshed, riot police, or your help.

Some think it's pretty important and will have a domino effect that will forever change the practice of country club memberships.

Before I go on, let me quickly remind you of a couple of your previous comments.

"Of course, if Shoal Creek lets blacks become members, they'd have to install separate drinking fountains and restrooms. Besides, where would the blacks ride? The golf bags already take up the back of the golf carts."

Sorry to break it to you, Woody, old boy, but no such thing has occurred. It was Hall Thompson himself who called Louis Willie to inform him of membership. And you might have heard that Willie took a few swings yesterday at Shoal Creek. I'm not even sure they had to call out the National Guard.

By the way, Woody, I tried to call you yesterday to share my views personally and let you know of our news.

But the woman who answered the phone at your newspaper had never heard of you. Maybe if you stuck to subjects in your own backyard, the folks at the newspaper would learn your name.

Anyway, she couldn't talk long. I think they were holding the front page for her story on the opening of a new yogurt shop in Ventura.

Speaking of your fair town, Wood-Man, let me also share another conversation I had yesterday with an official at the Ventura Chamber of Commerce. I'll provide you with an excerpt because I know a credible reporter like you would accept nothing less.

Just a couple of questions, please ma'am. First of all, how big is Ventura?

"Oh, it's pretty big, about 92,000."

For a visitor, what would the main attractions be?

"Main attractions. Uh, well, we have a beach."

Is there anyone famous who hails from Ventura?

"Famous? ... I don't know. I would imagine there might be one or two."

Any good restaurants?

"Oh, yes. We have three McDonald's. One on Telegraph, one on Victoria and the other on Harbor Boulevard."

Woody, sounds like you've got yourself one All-American town out there. I know with all the big-time sights and the major sports franchises in Ventura, it would be hard for you to get out of town for a little break. But if your boss could give you a few days off (hey, certainly he can find someone else to cover the Industrial Bowling League semifinals), I'd like to show you around Birmingham.

I'll make sure the Chamber of Commerce meets you at the airport and gives you the customary tar-and-feather kit all visitors receive upon arrival. Also, don't bother to eat on the plane. We have some excellent restaurants here.

In case you are hungry for some local Ventura cuisine, we have 27 McDonald's in the Birmingham area.

Even though I'm sure you command a huge salary at such a prestigious paper, let me insist on picking up the check. You can even order apple pie for dessert.

If I may indulge your patience, let me tell you a bit about our sports history.

Of course, you already know that Birmingham will play host to its second PGA Championship in six years.

I'm sure you also know we have had three NCAA Southeast Regional Finals here since 1982. I don't remember seeing Louisville, Indiana, UNLV, or Georgetown cutting down the nets at any tournament games at the Ventura YMCA gym.

I won't waste time with the number of major college football games in Birmingham each year that are broadcast nationally. Certainly, Ventura can match that.

And I'm sure Ventura is in the running for a WLAF franchise.

Hey, while you're here, you might want to take a look at the Alabama Sports Hall of Fame, where you can see busts of a couple minor-league sports stars such as Bear Bryant, Joe Namath, Bart Starr, Hank Aaron, and Joe Louis.

Certainly, Ventura has something like that for all of the famous people that have come through town.

I'd love to go on and on. But Woody, old buddy, time is short. It's nearly 1 p.m., so I must rush out to Shoal Creek in time to cover the daily cross-burning.

Sincerely,
(Your Pal) Paul

I tried to put a humorous spin on the Shoal Creek issue. Unfortunately, most of the laughter was being directed at us from the rest of the country.

August 7, 1990

Contrite Thompson holed up but he's holding up quite well

As the best golfers in the world teed off yesterday to play a practice round on the breathtaking masterpiece he carved out of Double Oak Mountain, Hall W. Thompson had just finished reading a letter from Gene Sarazen, the legendary golfer, urging the Shoal Creek founder to keep a stiff upper lip in the wake of the international controversy over the club's membership policies.

"Come on in," Thompson said, waving me into this office.

I had not seen Thompson since mid-June, the week before his infamous remarks to a *Birmingham Post-Herald* reporter. I wondered, like many, what effect the controversy might have on him.

Would he be depressed or despondent? Or would he be angry at the world?

For the most part, Thompson looked quite well. His handshake was firm. And as he walked around his desk to show me a seat, he looked pretty good for a 67-year-old man.

Oh, maybe a little tired. But under the circumstances, that certainly was understandable.

"You've gotten to be a pretty famous man around the world in the last few weeks," I told Thompson as I sat down. "I was in London last week, and there you were in every paper in Western Europe."

Thompson shook his head and laughed. He found it humorous when I mentioned that one of the London dailies had changed his name in a dispatch from Hall to Hal.

While Thompson was laughing on the outside, I wondered if deep down, in his heart of hearts, perhaps he was really crying.

This has been a trying time for him. Suddenly, because of a single comment—albeit an incredibly stupid one—he was thrust into the eye of a punishing hurricane.

Some men might have cracked, even become suicidal. But Thompson simply has gritted his teeth and taken the many painful and vicious lashes from the news media, among others—and survived.

There were no pickets yesterday. The National Guard didn't have to be called out.

Instead, Shoal Creek led the way for this nation's country clubs and now has a black member.

And there are more to come.

"I made a mistake, I know that," Thompson said. "And I deeply regret it."

It was clear to this reporter that Thompson really meant it. This was not some duplicitous remark, the kind you get from an Iraqi dictator.

"You have no idea how badly he has taken this," said a friend of Thompson's who asked not to be identified. "He feels he let his friends down, he feels he let everybody down. But he didn't. He has done so much for us. We're not going to abandon him over this. When someone else makes a mistake, people forget it.

"But when that someone is wealthy and successful like Hall Thompson, people don't want to accept his apology."

It probably would serve Thompson well to set the record straight publicly this week. Friends said he considered a press conference to do just that.

But he was advised it probably would turn into a circus. So instead, Thompson has chosen a less confrontational route: silence.

In certain respects, it is in keeping with his style.

Although he is known as a man not afraid to give his opinion, he prefers to stay in the background.

A few years ago, Thompson, along with Birmingham business magnate John Harbert, raised gobs of money to build the multipurpose facility known now as The Harbert Center.

"The original plan was to name it the Harbert-Thompson Center," a friend said. "But he didn't want any of the credit. He told them to forget it."

And even yesterday, now that the controversy has been settled, Thompson refused to stick his hand back in the frying pan.

"I'll be happy to talk about the tournament," Thompson said. "And the golf course. But there already has been enough said about the other."

As for the tournament, Thompson is predicting a winning score of 10-under par.

"I think 10-under will be a good score. The person who wins will have to keep it in the fairway."

As for Thompson's presence this week, there are some cowards with the PGA of America who would have preferred he be elsewhere. But Thompson's friends and family urged him to remain on the scene.

And rightfully so.

After all, this is his golf course, his home. Without Hall Thompson, the PGA would be in some hick town in Indiana this week. And the big story in Birmingham would be the Barons.

So Thompson decided to stick around. His official title is honorary chairman, but he'll still have his hand in the operation.

"I am exceptionally pleased with what they have done," said Thompson, referring to the work of his son, Mike, and Tom Hough, the tournament co-chairmen. "They have a great young team. It's just a shame this might be the last one we ever do."

With that, Thompson went silent. He probably had said more than he wanted to.

"I'm just looking forward to the week," Thompson said. "Unlike in 1984, I just want to enjoy this and maybe even see some golf."

Here is one person who hopes he does. No matter what Hall Thompson said or meant on that fateful day in June, he deserves to enjoy this championship. He has worked too long and hard to be deprived of that.

This was Hall Thompson's first interview since the Shoal Creek episode erupted into an international controversy. Although he didn't say much, The New York Times *and countless other papers across the world quoted from this column.*

AUGUST 29, 1990

Dream reveals the real Eddie Blake story

Forget all the controversy over Eddie Blake and how the 6-foot-4 310-pound junior college lineman—believed by some to be the best ever at his position—got into Auburn *without* a high school degree.

I had a dream last night and imagined this is the way it went down.

It was a dark, chilly February day during a recruiting weekend when Pat Dye's secretary waved Blake into the office.

Dye greeted him with a handshake.

"Eddie, we want you here at Auburn. You're the best in the country and we only want the best here."

"Well, coach, I've got this problem."

"What do you mean?"

"You see, Coach, I never graduated from high school."

"Well, Eddie, you seem like a smart young man to me. After all, you're presently enrolled at Northwest Mississippi Junior College and from what I'm told, that's one of the best junior colleges in the whole northwestern part of Mississippi."

"Yes sir, Coach. I'm really proud of my school."

"Now, Eddie, I want you to know that there is nothing more important to us here at Auburn than academics."

"You don't say, Coach."

"Well, nothing except beating Alabama's butt every year, which I don't mind telling you, we are doing with regularity. Of course, we're throwing them a little ol' bone this year by playing up in their sandbox. But last year, they had to come down here."

"Yep, I saw the game."

"You did. What did you think?"

"Well, I enjoyed it, but my college coach said you were pretty stupid to try that pass at the end of the game."

"Well, Eddie, you just worry about getting into Auburn and leave the coaching to me."

"I'm sorry. My coach also mentioned that he nearly busted a gut during the 1986 Alabama-Auburn game."

"Eddie, what did he find so amusing about that?"

"He said you looked pretty goofy trying to call a timeout at the end of the game while Lawyer Tillman was running that reverse in for the winning score ... And Coach, he also mentioned the 1984 game when Bo went...."

"Shut up, Eddie. Did it ever occur to your coach that if he spent more time worrying about his own job, he wouldn't be stuck coaching some podunk junior college in the backwoods of Mississippi?"

"Sorry, Coach."

"Now, did you call some of those former players I told you about to give you a better understanding of how things are done here at Auburn? "

"Yes sir, Coach. I talked to Jeff Burger and he gave me the name of a couple of people that might—well, you know—show me the ropes on writing term papers."

"What about the other names?"

"Yes sir, Coach. I also called Brent Fullwood. He sent me a couple of things in the mail."

"He did?"

"Yeah, Coach. He sent me an unopened Christmas present you had given him a few years back."

"I don't remember that."

"Well, Coach Dye, it was a map of how to get from the football dorm to his 8:05 a.m. class. He also sent me the Sony Walkman you gave him which included the audio-walking tour with the three best shortcuts across campus from Domino's Pizza to the undergraduate library.

"Well, enough of all that. From the look of things, we are going to have to give you some special testing because of this high school degree thing."

"OK by me, Coach. But you know that you don't have to have a high school degree to get into junior college. All you need is a GED."

"Of course, I know that, Eddie. Do you think I'm some kind of idiot?"

"Uh ... no sir."

"OK Eddie, how are you in math?"

"Pretty good, Coach."

"Now, Eddie, I'm going to pull out these flashcards here and within one second, give me the answer. Now, what is 25 times 5?"

"Why, that's 125, Coach."

"Very good, very quick. I like that in a lineman ... Well, Eddie enough of all this here testing. You seem like a fine young man. And from what I hear, you're about the best lineman to come out in many moons. So consider yourself enrolled."

"Well, Coach, I certainly appreciate the opportunity. And I won't let you down. I hope everybody just lets me forget about the past."

"Eddie, I couldn't agree with you more. Ain't no sense in looking back at all that stuff. Leave that to those pinheads in the press."

"Right, Coach."

"Eddie, let me finish our meeting by telling you something my momma and daddy used to tell me ... and one Sue and I always tell our own chilluns."

"What's that Coach?"

"Just don't worry about the past because hindsight is always 50-50."

"Coach, no disrespect, intended. But hindsight is 20-20."

"Listen, Eddie, you let me worry about that stuff. You just worry about staying in school and beating Alabama ... and not necessarily in that order."

I simply tried to put a funny spin on the Eddie Blake story. Auburn fans didn't find it very funny. Of course, Auburn fans don't find anything funny.

DECEMBER 5, 1990

Perkins's firing a sad moment

Once upon a time (and not all that long ago), I would have thrown a lavish party upon hearing the news that Ray Perkins had been fired.

But when the story moved on the wire early Monday afternoon that Tampa Bay Buccaneers owner Hugh Culverhouse finally had pulled the plug on Perkins, there was no feeling of exhilaration. Instead, I was sad because Perkins really deserved a better fate.

Say what you want about this peculiar 49-year-old football coach. But don't tell me he can't coach football.

Perkins had put together the makings of a very good football team in Tampa Bay. Of course, it wasn't good enough for Culverhouse.

Then again, Culverhouse never has been known for his football acumen.

This is the guy who stayed with John McKay so long you could smell the mildew on the former USC coach. This is the guy who hired a reject like Leeman Bennett when he could have had anyone.

Who can forget Culverhouse's bungling of the Bo Jackson affair? It should have been the foundation for the backward franchise. Instead, Culverhouse fumbled and stumbled and before you could say "Bo knows football," Jackson was in the Kansas City Royals outfield playing baseball.

This is the same Culverhouse, the same honorable and decent man, who lied a few weeks ago when he said he wouldn't fire Perkins even if he lost every remaining game this season.

So much for a vote of confidence (or should it really have been called a kiss of death?).

That is not to say Perkins didn't make his own bed. He blew it by moving quarterback Vinny Testaverde out of the starting lineup.

Still, the Bucs slowly were coming around. But Culverhouse ran out of patience. The fans screamed "boycott," and Culverhouse became weak in the knees and jerked the Perk.

Yes, Perkins's personality, that much-maligned aspect of this man we came to know (and occasionally hate) at Alabama, also got the better of him in Tampa.

The fans couldn't stand the man, which was nothing new.

Earlier this year, a reporter asked Perkins to comment on the way he conducts business.

"I make the decisions, and I can live by them, you know," Perkins said. "And I don't give a damn what anybody thinks. That's just the way I am. I've always been that way.

"Sometimes I don't do things the American way, but sometimes the American way stinks. I'm not part of the American way. I don't know why I am the way I am. I'm serious.

"Sometimes I wonder if it's worth being honest and doing what I think is right. The American way is to lie. The American way is to say things that people want to hear. Part of the

American way is politics, and I think politics is part of the reason this country is in the shape it's in."

Despite the rhetoric, Perkins was a very caring and decent person. He gave hundreds of thousands of dollars to charity. He helped abused and homeless children. He helped anyone who asked.

He remained loyal to Alabama. During the Bill Curry years, Perkins fielded many calls from his former players, unhappy with the regime. He made a special trip last January to Alabama to congratulate Gene Stallings on getting the Alabama job.

This is the side of Perkins few people saw. I failed to see it (perhaps a better excuse is I didn't look very hard) until after he was gone.

So now what?

Perkins says he wants to remain in coaching—preferably in the college game. Would a two-Mercedes family such as the Perkinses want to live in Starkville, Mississippi?

When you think about Perkins's legacy, I think mostly of the two words, "What if?"

What if Perkins never had left the New York Giants for Alabama?

It is possible Perkins would have been on the sideline Monday night coaching the New York Giants, a team that still has his imprint some nine years later?

What if Perkins had not left Alabama in 1987 for Tampa Bay?

The guess here is there would be a couple of Southeastern Conference championship rings on his hand that now are worn by Auburn coach Pat Dye.

As a college coach, Perkins was a tad conservative for my taste. But he may have been one of the finest recruiters I've seen in college football.

Finally, what if Bill Curry had not fled Tuscaloosa for the bluer grass of Kentucky?

If Curry had remained at Alabama—and struggled this year and lost to Auburn (two strong possibilities!)—Perkins would have been at the top of any list to replace him.

Another irony is Richard Williamson, who lost to Stallings for the Alabama job, has taken over for Perkins on an interim basis. Had Curry stayed, the man who might be the interim coach in Tampa could have been Stallings.

After Stallings was fired in Phoenix, Perkins offered to hire him at Tampa. Stallings might have taken the job if ... .

Today, Stallings probably is one of the most popular men in Alabama and Perkins is out of work.

Funny how things work out.

But they are not funny for Ray Perkins. He deserved better. Hopefully, he will find it somewhere else.

After this column, you're probably wondering about me. Could Finebaum be schizophrenic? I just wanted to say it before you could. Interestingly, after Perkins moved back to Alabama, he spent the 1991 football season as a weekly analyst on my radio show. I quickly found out unemployment did nothing to change Perkins's personality. You could still catch a cold sitting next to him.

MARCH 2, 1991

Sometimes, the teacher can learn from the kids

In the last few months, I have spoken to a myriad of groups, from Rotary to Quarterback Clubs, to high school assemblies to college seminars.

I can honestly say I've enjoyed them all. Some more than others. But often, it is difficult, preparing a talk, delivering it, trying to be informative and witty. All of this while keeping my eyes open for incoming Scuds, usually in the form of rotten tomatoes or eggs from the disgruntled Alabama or Auburn fans in the audience.

But the other day, I found myself in a setting unlike any other.

I was invited to speak to a couple of third-grade classes at Clay Elementary School. I was a little apprehensive. I have no children of my own (yet).

So I checked in with my 5-year-old nephew—my main source on such pressing issues—to get the latest gossip on Mario and Raphael and Slimer and the Ninja Turtles and Big Bird and, of course, the Bart-Man.

After all, I wanted to be cool speaking to a group of 8 and 9-year-olds. I didn't want to sound square. After all, I am in my thirties.

I thought it would be tough, though. I didn't figure many third-graders read the newspaper. I know the *Weekly Reader* is hot. However, I didn't know about the *Birmingham Post-Herald*.

Nor did I think these kids would know me from Norman Schwarzkopf.

To my surprise, they knew a lot about sports and everything else.

After reading them a children's story (I think it was the wolf's inside story of the "The Three Little Pigs,") I invited the youngsters to ask questions.

To my surprise nearly every one of them raised their hands.

One of the first questions was about my job.

"Have you ever been to an Alabama-Auburn game?" asked a little girl.

When I told her that not only do I go to it every year, that I get a 50-yard-line seat, get to sip on a Pepsi during the game, and don't get rained on—all of that while being paid—the group nearly came undone.

"You get paid to go to football games!" she said, incredulously.

But the group of third-graders was even more surprised and shocked to learn that I actually knew some of the people who coach and play in those games.

"I bet you don't know Bo Jackson," said one little boy.

When I informed him that not only do I know Bo, that I have interviewed him (although not very recently), the youngsters just shook their heads in disbelief.

They asked about the Birmingham Fire and seemed more interested in Torch, the fire-breathing mascot than Brent Pease, the top-rated quarterback.

One boy asked me about George Bush.

When I mentioned that I had met Bush before, they nearly came unglued.

Bo may know Bo. But these kids were far more impressed with George Bush than Bo Jackson.

"Next time you see him," one boy said, "tell him to get Saddam Hussein for me." I assured him I would pass along the message.

At the end of the session, the teachers asked the group to stand and sing me a song they were preparing for an assembly later in the week.

They all rose and sang a stirring rendition of Lee Greenwood's "God Bless the USA."

Some were out of key. A few were quite creative when it came to the actual words.

But it got me thinking back to another time, another elementary school, one I went to in the sixties.

It was a different era, one where the newspapers showed pictures on the front of flags burning. However, back then, it was the stars and stripes—not the Iraqi flag—going up in flames.

People sang songs about America during the sixties. But many were not patriotic.

And now here I was, listening to third-graders singing and smiling about our victory in the Persian Gulf. I could feel tears well in my eyes from happiness and joy.

I had gone to Clay Elementary School to be the teacher, to read a story and answer questions, to help educate youngsters about today's world.

But a funny thing happened this week when I went back to school.

I was the one who had learned.

This column was somewhat out of character for a curmudgeon like me, but I had such a good time visiting the children and I felt compelled to write about it.

June 8, 1991

Sour grapes, Mark? Atlanta not so peachy

Just when you thought the Atlanta-Birmingham battle over the Southeastern Conference championship football game was over and done, out from under a slimy and insect-infested rock crawls Mark Bradley, a sports columnist for *The Atlanta Constitution*.

Some of you sports junkies might remember Bradley from his former job as Bill Curry's chief hatchetman during the former Alabama coach's reign in Tuscaloosa.

Bradley was to Curry what Rabbi Baruch Korff was to Richard Nixon in his final days.

So Birmingham-bashing is nothing new for Bradley, who was born and bred in the Bluegrass state. Here is a man who was taught at an early age that all Alabamians were named Bubba or Earl and chewed tobacco after meals instead of flossing.

But yesterday, in his column, he took his hatred of our town to new depths. He gave what he thought were the reasons why the SEC chose Birmingham over Atlanta.

Wrote Bradley:

"In Atlanta, the choice of chic night life ranges from Rupert's to Velvet to Petrus. A visitor to Birmingham faces no such dilemma. Over there, everybody just congregates at the Shoney's breakfast bar ... .

"At first some coaches were concerned they might have to face Alabama in Birmingham for the SEC title. But upon reviewing tapes of the Tide's 27-point loss to Louisville in the Fiesta Bowl, those same coaches decided that playing a Gene Stallings team in post season mightn't be such a bad deal."

Other gems included:

• "Holding an event in Birmingham is a surefire way of generating publicity. Remember how big the PGA went over at Shoal Creek."

• "So what if Atlanta is the headquarters of CNN. Birmingham now has cable."

• "Folks in Alabama know how to liven up a dull game: Break out the water cannon and hose down your visitors."

• "Tourists sometimes have to wait in line at Atlanta restaurants. In Birmingham, the best places all have drive-thrus."

• "Wanting to cast its lot with an international city, the SEC looked past the cheap sensationalism of the 1996 Olympics and focused entirely upon Birmingham, which plays host to a truly venerable institution—the WLAF."

After reading the column, I began thinking about all of the wonderful attractions Atlanta has to offer.

Here is a partial list of some of the things the SEC missed out on by not taking the title game to that city:

• Guided tours of the prison cell block housing convicted child-serial killer Wayne Williams.

• A visit to the world-famous Varsity restaurant, whose chili dogs, cheeseburgers, and fried onion rings are so tasty, the management is believed to offer a money-back guarantee to any customer who doesn't come down with dysentery in 12 hours.

• Get the three-for-one tour of the birthplaces of J. B. Stoner, Lester Maddox, and Newt Gingrich, the three Georgians whose political philosophy most closely resembles that of Benito Mussolini.

• Take a guided tour of where Ted Turner and Jane Fonda live and stop outside to salute the North Vietnamese flag flying in front of the lawn.

• Take a side trip to the state mental institution to visit the architect who designed the Atlanta interstate system.

• Of course, you could always travel to College Park and visit the birthplace of Curry, the Atlanta resident who has picked up right where P. T. Barnum left off.

• Visit a souvenir shop and buy your choice of bumper stickers reading: "Atlanta: Murder Capital of the USA" or the other hot-seller, "Atlanta: The Newark of the South."

• If you have 30 extra minutes, you can take the Grey Line bus tour out to Forsyth County and watch wives of City Council members wash their husband's Klan sheets.

• Tour the Atlanta wax museum of famous citizens, such as Bill Carter posing with his famous beer. The hottest exhibit, however, is the one of Atlanta's best-known columnist, Lewis Grizzard, posing with his favorite food and drink: a moon pie and an RC Cola.

This one did not make me any friends in Atlanta. But then again, I don't have any friends in Birmingham, either.

JUNE 15, 1991

True injustice is that Ramsey thinks he's right

The Eric Ramsey case is so sad because this young man actually believes Pat Dye is a racist.

Either that, or someone has told him what to believe.

There are bigots and racists and closet-Klan members in every office and probably on every athletic staff in the South.

But I can tell you one thing: Patrick Fain Dye isn't one of them.

If anything, he has been one of the greatest champions of black athletes to come down the pike in a long time.

When Proposition 48 came to pass several years ago, Dye was the one who screamed the loudest and raised the most cain.

He did the same thing when Proposition 42—even tougher legislation that some believed was aimed at blacks—was put into effect.

As a result of his stand, Dye has been severely criticized from some pointy-headed professors on the Auburn campus, who have nothing better to do than create trouble.

When the story came out that Brent Fullwood, a black player, was allowed to play in a bowl game after revelations he had not attended class in a month of Sundays, Dye defended the young man.

It would have been a popular decision to toss Fullwood off the bus. To say, "See you later, Alligator. I don't need you around no more."

But Dye stood firm.

Why?

Because, in Dye's words, Fullwood had given four years of life to Auburn football and deserved to play in the bowl game.

Although Dye's record on academics has been severely criticized, because of Fullwood and Jeff Burger and others, few coaches push players harder to graduate. He tells them repeatedly the door leading out of football can be dark and dank and full of unhappy surprises.

He is also colorblind.

Where many schools in the SEC have struggled with black quarterbacks—for a variety of reasons—Auburn under Dye has prospered. Pat Washington had some problems as Auburn's starting quarterback. But it had nothing to do with his being black. He became a graduate assistant under Dye before heading to Southwest Louisiana.

Reggie Slack led the Tigers to the SEC crown. Both have kind things to say about the Auburn program.

But not Ramsey.

Why has he gone public? Why has he struck so hard and with so much force against a program that provided him with a free education, free room and board, and an opportunity not only to graduate but play pro ball?

Did someone put Ramsey up to it?

Only Ramsey can answer that.

But one thing is for sure: his story has holes the size of Jupiter. He talks about segregation at the Auburn dorm. But Ramsey hasn't lived there since he was a freshman.

He is now married; he is a father. He charges his fellow players treated him like an outcast as a result. I'm sure there was some truth to it. But was it because he was black? Or was it because he was married and a father among a group of teenagers, some of whose interests were beating Alabama and chasing women—and not necessarily in that order?

Ramsey describes his time at Auburn as "a living hell." If it were so bad, if he were discriminated against because he was black, why did he wait until his career was over to tell history?

If things were so intolerable, why didn't he pick up the phone and call Reverend Abraham Woods?

Something tells me Ramsey would not have had to wait long for the call to be returned.

Ramsey says someone had to come clean on this problem.

"If I have to be the Martin Luther King of this generation, I will be," Ramsey said.

Unfortunately, if Ramsey were a student of the slain civil rights leader, his statements about racism would have had some meat and clarity.

If Auburn's football program is racist, if it is condescending to blacks, there is work to do and serious problems to solve.

But something tells me the biggest problem with racism at Auburn right now exists primarily in the mind of Eric Ramsey.

That is the tragedy of this story.

This appeared after Ramsey's first allegations, which involved charges of racism. He saved his best stuff for later. This was one of those columns where I imitated the Los Angeles police. I shot first and asked questions later.

NOVEMBER 13, 1991

Magic doesn't fit definition of hero

Since announcing publicly that he has tested HIV positive, the precursor of the virulent AIDS virus, Magic Johnson has been referred to as "a great hero" by everyone from George Bush on down.

And yesterday, Bush even invited Johnson to join the National Commission on AIDS.

Certainly, Johnson's performance on the basketball court is legendary. So are the countless hours and millions of dollars he has helped raise for charitable causes.

Like millions of Americans, I feel bad for him, and hope Johnson can beat the almost impossible odds he now faces.

But the nagging question remains: Is Magic Johnson the hero that President Bush—and many in this country—want to make him out to be?

Regrettably, he is not.

Hero is a big word and one of the most badly misused nouns in the English language. Heroes are men and women who participated on the streets of America the other day in Veterans Day celebrations. Men and women with no arms or legs being pushed in wheelchairs, still smiling, still waving the flag of the red, white, and blue for which they fought.

A hero is a young kid like Ryan White, an innocent victim of the AIDS virus.

Magic Johnson should not be called a hero simply because he has contracted AIDS and stepped forward to admit it.

To be an effective spokesman, Johnson needs to adjust his message and hopefully he will.

Johnson has not talked of the error of his behavior. Instead, he has seemingly taken a cavalier attitude that he lost a numbers game while failing to practice safe sex.

Unfortunately, this is a flawed message.

Before little kids looked up to Magic Johnson, they looked up (even higher) at Wilt Chamberlain.

Now, we find that while we were craning our necks to applaud Chamberlain, he was rattling box springs as well as backboards.

In his newly released book, *A View From Above*, Chamberlain said: "If I had to count my sexual encounters, I would be closing in on 20,000 different ladies." Before you break out the pocket calculator, that averages out to 1.2 women per day since he reached puberty.

I guess, you could say, that not only was Chamberlain the NBA's scoring leader on the court—but off it as well.

Until Earvin "Magic" Johnson.

When some media reports earlier this week attempted to link Johnson to the Los Angeles gay community, his agent, Lon Rosen, denied it, saying:

"The reason nothing like this has ever surfaced is because Magic's one of the biggest ladies' men of our time. He's in the trouble he's in today because he took it to extremes. He just hopes everyone he's had contact with is taking a test."

Well, certainly, that is considerate of Magic, now isn't it?

Peter Vescey of *USA Today*, perhaps the closest follower of the NBA in the business, wrote:

"At the same time as much as I'm shocked, I'm not shocked. Magic's promiscuous bachelor lifestyle these last dozen years—I doubt he has ever heard the word 'no'—left him brutally exposed ... Even in this day and age of AIDS, an awful lot of players pass around the same women in every city ...."

The truth of the matter is Johnson is now suffering the consequences of his promiscous behavior. He has not admitted his moral failings. Instead, on the Arsenio Hall show the other night, he preached safe sex, stating that the youth of America need to "put on their thinking cap and a cap down there."

While this may sound hip, it is not the right message.

There are grave consequences of delivering such a message, which puts youths in the dangerous position of exposure to the AIDS virus.

"There is no such thing as safe sex," said Dr. Samford Kuvin of the National Foundation of Infectious Disease. "There is safer sex using a condom, but condoms slip, rip, crack, and leak."

By delivering such a message, Johnson is stereotyping young people in general—and specifically blacks—in effect saying they cannot control their sexual drives.

Johnson can still be a hero in this battle. He can do so by admitting the behavior leading up to this condition was morally wrong.

And for the sake of American youth, he can change his message from promoting "safe sex" to promoting that sex outside of marriage is wrong.

Then, you could call Magic Johnson a hero.

The genesis of this column came from a conversation with a close friend, Reverend Tom Caradine of Briarwood Presbyterian Church. I received more mail on this article than any other in my career. For weeks, volumes of mail piled up, all but a handful of letters praising the column. The letters came from all over the country, since the column, through the syndicate wire, appeared in many newspapers around the nation. I still can't believe I wrote something this intelligent.

FEBRUARY 12, 1992

Shed no tears for this bum

This time, Mike Tyson's fists couldn't do the talking. This time, 12 folks from Indiana made the decision, instead of three stooges dressed up like penguins, scoring the decision on compassion instead of malevolence.

To some observers, the verdict in the rape trial of boxer Mike Tyson was stunning. However, to those who felt that way, it was obvious they had absorbed too much of the William Kennedy Smith trial and Clarence Thomas hearings, where the accused men beat the rap. This time, the fat lady sung for the man.

For many years, Tyson has been an accident waiting to happen. Actually, there have been several major crashes on Tyson's crooked highway of life. But this time, Tyson's brutal uppercut and punishing left hook—which have only failed him once in a storied professional career—weren't enough to outdistance the law.

Shed no tears for this convicted rapist, this common criminal. Tyson is a bum; an animal disguised under human flesh. He probably deserves the electric chair but those familiar with Indiana law predict he won't get any more than six to ten.

Hopefully, there will be something positive to come out of this. Not so much that Tyson is put behind bars. But instead, let's hope this jury verdict will send a stern message to any other athlete/celebrity types that if they continue to treat women like dirt, they may soon be digging it up on a prison chain gang.

In the wake of this verdict, some in the media will round up the usual suspects who claim Tyson never had a chance—that he was a victim of a poor background, where violence was part of the texture and tapestry of his existence.

But as folks in these parts are so fond of saying: That dog won't hunt.

While it is true Tyson grew up in a frightening Brooklyn ghetto, he was able to break out only to become one of the most famous, richest atheletes in the world.

But designer suits and designer cologne could not eviscerate the stench of Tyson's demonic soul. He was nothing but a two-bit punk masquerading in a grown-up's body.

Tyson had the best cars and homes. His handlers nightly rounded up the best bimbos for him.

But money couldn't destroy the cancer spreading in his body.

Only when Tyson fought in the ring was the world safe from the boxer. Then, only his opponent could be brutally punished. But unlike an 18-year-old girl, the opponent was being paid to take the beating.

Some hair spray idiot on television the other day asked if this whole affair hasn't given boxing a black eye. How can a sport which already is the sleaziest, most corrupt and barbaric of all, be hurt by another black eye?

Boxing will go on with or without Tyson. Perhaps, it will be better off without him.

Several years ago, Tyson was asked about his philosophy on fighting.

"When I fight someone, I want to break his will. I want to take his manhood. I want to rip out his heart and show it to him.... People says that's primitive, that I'm an animal. But then, they pay $500 to see it. There's so much hypocrisy in the world."

Tyson is right about the hypocrisy part. But, at least, we have a judicial system, one that attempts to put criminals in their place.

Few men in recent history have looked better in a boxing ring. But something tells me Tyson will look even more at home in a jail cell.

In that setting, Mike Tyson will be caged in and treated like the animal he has proven to be.

I must admit that with Tyson's parole coming up, I am concerned. What if he reads this and decides to look me up? On second thought, I doubt Tyson can read.

April 11, 1992

Coupleses make quite a couple

AUGUSTA—Unlike politics, where wives are often pushed to the front of the stage by overzealous handlers for the perfunctory kiss, the spouses of professional golfers normally stay in the background.

Oh, Barbara Nicklaus is usually seen following in the paw prints of her husband, the Golden Bear.

But never—and I mean never—has the golfing world seen anything quite like Deborah Couples.

The blond-headed, statuesquely built wife of the world's No. 1 player has drawn almost as many raves from the galleries this week as her husband, Fred, whose sizzling 67 yesterday has him a single stroke behind leaders Craig Parry and Ian Woosnam at The Masters.

Deborah first burst on the scene back in 1983, when her husband won the Kemper Open. Instead of calmly walking out to the green for the customary kiss, Deborah, wearing a cowboy hat and a rather snug hot-pink outfit, sprinted. She then leaped into Couples arms in a scene which closely resembled the kind you see between a catcher and a pitcher following the deciding game of the World Series.

The rather staid and snotty golfing world had never seen anything quite like it.

Since then, she has been a favorite of golfing galleries everywhere.

While her husband was speaking to the international media late yesterday afternoon about his stunning round, there was Deborah in the back of the room, gabbing away with several reporters.

Outrageously dressed in a white fish-net outfit, she (needless to say) turned a few heads among the male-dominated members of the news media.

In less than a minute, she had wiggled both feet loose from her shoes and walked around in only stocking feet.

Barbara Nicklaus probably would have fainted on the spot.

When Couples finished, she scampered to meet him in the back of the press tent—not to hug his neck and fawn over the world's hottest golfer. Instead, she needed to borrow some money from her husband, who has already won $738,162 this season.

"I need to go to Kroger's and buy some groceries for dinner," said Deborah. "I'm going to fix him some angel-hair pasta with marinara sauce. I think I'll also do some eggplant. Maybe, some Haagen-Dazs for dessert."

Deborah and Fred are basically homebodies.

Freddie's favorite passion isn't golf. But, instead, watching television.

"Fred and I would be happy if nobody ever asked another question," Deborah said. "We just like to hang."

Of course, Deborah likes to do a few other things, such as play tennis and polo.

She grew up in Texas and met her husband while he played for the University of Houston. They have no children.

Deborah played briefly on the Virginia Slims Pro Tennis Tour. She now teaches tennis but prefers to play polo.

"Fred and I just are very casual," Deborah said. "I don't want our lives to change just because his golf has improved."

Deborah said there is no evidence Couples plays any better with her around.

"I think he plays well both ways," she said, in a classic understatement. "But he enjoys having me out there."

"I don't go to all of the tournaments anymore because of tennis, polo, and my design business. I have a lot going on. And I just don't think I could do it, anyway. I'm not putting anybody down who does, but I would go absolutely, raving-mad and I would drive him crazy, besides."

With Couples's spectacular success, some people have quietly suggested she tone her act down.

"I would be a terrible political wife," Deborah said. "I kind of shoot from the hip. Someone told me I'm going to have to (tone down) now that Fred is No. 1. But he never tells me not to talk. He gets a kick out of me."

And Deborah quickly pointed out that their lives will not change at all if Couples fails to win The Masters.

"We don't have to win this thing," Deborah said. "Life will definitely go on."

With that, her waiting husband waved her away from this reporter.

"Let's go," said Fred Couples.

And they were quickly gone.

After all, the evening was still young. There were groceries to buy and television to watch.

After this column, some of my friends (both of them), accused me of having an affair with Deborah Couples during the Masters. Those suspicions intensified several months later when the Couples' couple broke up and were divorced. For the real story on this, you'll have to buy my next book.

APRIL 15, 1992

Remember Ashe for way he lived

Arthur Ashe will be laid to rest today in his native Virginia. But it won't stop the eulogies and tributes that continue to come in from every corner of the globe. The messages have been delivered by presidents and kings, by corporate executives and street cleaners.

Ashe had that effect on people. He was a quiet but brilliant man, whose soft voice resonated throughout the sporting world.

It was Ashe who once said of black people: "I have become conviced that we blacks spend too much time on the playing field and too little in the libraries."

Comments such as that upset people. But Ashe believed you had to do that sometimes to make your point heard.

Unfortunately, mention of so many of Ashe's greatest accomplishments will be dimmed now becaue of his battle with AIDS.

The illness has become the centerpiece of Ashe's life and career instead of his many outstanding accomplishments and contributions.

While the AIDS battle is an immensly important cause, hopefully his death will not overshadow his brilliant career. You might call Ashe a reluctant hero of this movement, which has taken on a certain political correctness in our society.

Some people believed the pushing by AIDS activists and others for Ashe's time and energy might have accelerated his demise.

Dr. Henry Murray, Ashe's personal physician, is quoted by *The New York Times* as saying he was surprised by the sudden death of the tennis champion.

The doctor said even a few hours before his death, when Ashe's breathing had to be assisted by a respirator, the feeling was he would recover.

Did the stress and pressure shorten the span of his life?

Certainly, physicians say those are two things that people who have the disease—or any serious malady—should try to avoid.

His final year of life was hardly lived the way this quiet, private man would have planned it. The public disclosure of his illness began in April when a *USA Today* reporter confronted him. Although Ashe had known about his illness for years, he had not made a public disclosure.

Subsequent to the announcement, he became an important spokesman for AIDS.

At first, Ashe was angry as a result of being forced to admit he had the virulent disease. However, being the true champion that he is, he realized a crisis often was the road to opportunity.

His close friends said he turned the public airing of his illness into one of the most productive periods of his life.

However, this was not the road orginally chosen by Ashe.

Nor does one really believe it is the legacy he wished to leave for his family and friends.

Yet, in today's world, the battle with AIDS seems to have take precedent over all other diseases.

While one cannot fault Ashe for giving his time and energy to the movement, did he really have a choice?

Ashe had been aware of his infection since 1988 and did not disclose it publicly. Now, with the announcement, the astute tennis champion perhaps concluded there would be no choice but to publicly join the battle against AIDS.

That might be the ultimate tragedy of Ashe's legacy. Because of the newspaper reporter and as a result of the peer pressure in our society to be politically correct, Ashe became a reluctant hero of the AIDS movement.

And now he is gone.

In every story about his death, the word AIDS is prominently mentioned although it is a narrow part of his legacy.

Last spring, after he went public, Ashe said: "I'm not a hero. I'm not anything but a man."

Hopefully, the AIDS activists will allow the world to remember that there is more to this great man's life than his death.

Although this came close on the heels of the Magic Johnson announcement, I felt compelled to deal with the AIDS issure one more time. Arthur Ashe died in January of 1993.

MAY 16, 1992

Toast of Tuscaloosa now just simply toast

Unfortunately in life, how you exit the stage is how you are best remembered. If there is a real tragedy in the saga of Alabama basketball coach Wimp Sanderson, that might be it.

When Woody Hayes's name is mentioned in general conversation, people don't discuss the great football players and championships the late Ohio State coach had in his 28-year career. Instead, they remember the final chapter ending with a punch.

There always is an apposition in a sentence about Hayes. Nobody just says Woody Hayes. Instead, it is Woody Hayes whose career ended in disgrace ... .

So now, so sadly, the same probably will be true for Sanderson.

He is the winningest coach in Alabama history, as well as the most popular. But wherever Sanderson goes from now on, people will talk behind his back and mention the alleged incident with his secretary. The gossip about Sanderson will echo, some of it sounding as if it had been lifted off the pages of the *National Enquirer*.

Scores of Wimp Sanderson jokes will make the rounds.

Meanwhile, the accomplishments of his brilliant coaching career at Alabama lay scattered across the terrain, like burned-out remnants of an airplane crash.

It has happened so dramatically, with such force, it is still difficult to catch one's breath and digest the news.

Journalists love a good story. The bigger and badder and sleazier and seamier it gets, usually the more we like it.

But I don't know any decent journalist who has enjoyed covering this story. It has been a painfully difficult and personally troubling process.

I've known Sanderson and been friendly with him for more than a decade. I have played in golf outings with him and helped raise money for charity alongside him.

While I feel badly for him, I also believe Sanderson's fall from grace has been coming for some time. As Sanderson grew in stature and popularity, so did his arrogance and paranoia. Very little ever seemed to satisfy Sanderson or really make him happy.

But something must have gone very wrong to have precipitated the events that led to these final, dark days.

Certainly allegations that he struck longtime administrative assistant Nancy Watts are at the core of his expected termination from the university. But one has to believe there is much more to the story than an isolated event in his office.

So what will happen to Sanderson? Can he get another job coaching?

One would have to think the answer is unlikely. Coaches have come back after after allegations of NCAA violations. But this is different. This is that gray area, that dead zone, from which college administrators normally shy away, especially in our politically charged environment.

The NBA, which will hire anybody (see Jerry Tarkanian) probably would not be interested in Sanderson.

What about becoming a color commentator on television?

This unquestionably is an area that has interested Sanderson for some time. Officials at Jefferson-Pilot said recently Sanderson did a test for them approximately one year ago.

Sanderson would be a natural for television. He is funny and glib.

Still, at least right now, networks might be nervous about hiring Sanderson.

Of course, this story is tragic for many people. One can't help but feel terribly sorry for Sanderson's wife and family. To sit by and have to watch and listen to all that's being said about him—both publicly and privately—must be like living through a nightmare.

One must also feel sorry for Watts. A little more than a week ago, she was unknown to the world. Now, in some people's eyes she has become the Anita Hill of Alabama.

Assistant coaches and their families must face the uncertainties in the days ahead and the players, the lifeblood of a basketball program, will be without their coach.

There are few certainties in the saga. Much is still not known.

But one thing seems certain. There are no winners. Everyone has lost something.

The fall of Sanderson was difficult for me because I (had) always liked the basketball coach.

MAY 20, 1992

Wimp's exit a circus act, not a class act

Someone put it best yesterday when he described the defiant departure of Alabama's basketball coach as "classic Wimp Sanderson" instead of "classy Wimp Sanderson."

It could have been so different. The end of a brilliant 32-year career that spanned millions of memories could have been poignant and graceful and handled with dignity. But instead of leaving with his head held high, Sanderson took the low road home.

Coach Paul "Bear" Bryant, whose name Sanderson evoked during his final day on the job, always lectured his players to "show some class" in defeat as well as in victory.

Apparently, Sanderson must have missed that statement while zipping through the quick-fix Bear quote book on the way to his resignation announcement. Instead of using it as a time of reflection, Sanderson turned his final day at Alabama into a circus.

One would think even Sanderson's staunchest supporters would concede his public show of carrying his boxes and plaid sports coats to his van in clear view of the television cameras and reporters was a cheap grandstanding move.

Then came this Sanderson's statement to the news media: "In no way do I feel this decision is justified or fair—and I'll fight it to my dying day."

That was followed by a humiliating second statement in which he praised Alabama athletic director Hootie Ingram.

Why did he reverse fields so quickly and dramatically? There are 394,854 reasons.

If Sanderson believed he was being mistreated, why did he agree to resign? He could have let the university fire him and attempt to settle the matter in court.

He also might have slipped in a denial of the allegations somewhere in the process. So far, no denial has been offered, although the word itself describes the mood of the moment.

Several officials in Tuscaloosa this week conceded that Sanderson was the last person in town to realize he was gone. As late as the middle of last week—nearly seven days after allegations that Sanderson struck a female subordinate first became public and nearly two months after the alleged incident—Sanderson was said to believe he would hold on to his job.

Apparently, he never fully realized the enormity of the allegations of giving his secretary a black eye. He didn't understand that *he* now had a black eye. He apparently didn't understand how the alleged incident might be used against him in recruiting, how it would be used against the basketball program in general.

Oh, there was a simple way to remove the dark, lingering cloud over the basketball program. The only way it could be done was for Sanderson to issue a denial.

Of course, Sanderson never did come forward with a denial or even an apology. All he said was the decision to fire him was unfair and unjustified.

It was clear that some of Sanderson's earlier shots were aimed at Ingram. While I am not here to present Sanderson and Ingram as bosom buddies, there is little convincing evidence the athletic director's fingerprints were on the murder weapon.

More than likely, you'll find that the man who pulled the trigger was school president Roger Sayers.

Of course, on the day the last shots were fired, Sayers was too busy cutting a ribbon at a groundbreaking, while Ingram was on live television pronouncing Sanderson's career over.

So we move on from here. The Sanderson era ends, and a search for a new man begins.

Late Monday, someone asked me if anyone could replace Sanderson at Alabama. After all, the person said, he *was* Alabama basketball.

Indeed, he was. He was bigger than life. But so was another fellow Sanderson is fond of quoting. Even now, a decade after his death, Coach Bryant is sorely missed at Alabama. But the football program has survived.

The Alabama basketball program will do the same without Wimp Sanderson.

The day of his resignation, Sanderson glared at me as he walked to his car. I actually thought he might hit me. He didn't and we haven't spoken since. For both, I am grateful.

AUGUST 15, 1992

Tourney fitting memorial for Bruno

When the question was first broached, his dark, brooding eyes turned glassy. He seemed to be biting his lip, holding back an explosion of emotion. Then, slowly and now composed, Ronnie Bruno began talking about his late father, Angelo.

"That's the major regret that I have about this tournament," Bruno was saying now, carefully measuring every word as he spoke. "The major regret is that he's not here."

Of the tens of thousands of fans who have visited or will visit Greystone Golf Club this week, the person who would have enjoyed it the most was Angelo Bruno.

Even though a tragic plane crash in December ended the lives of Bruno, his brother, Lee, and several key company employees, these men have not been forgotten during this special weekend in August.

Especially for those who loved them the most.

"I walked out to No. 1 (yesterday) to watch Lee Trevino tee off and I saw the crowd," Ronnie Bruno said. "The bleachers were full, and the fairways were lined with people.

"I said, 'God, I wish he could be here to see this.' Then, I thought I'm sure he is. The one consoling thought I have is that I know he's pleased with what we're doing. I'm sure that, somewhere, he is very happy about this."

It was difficult to listen to Ronnie Bruno talk about his father and not be choked up.

Ronnie Bruno might be the chairman of one of the largest and most important companies in the state. But one of his closest friends described him recently as an intensely private person. Some even go so far as to call him shy.

That wasn't difficult to believe yesterday morning as we sat off in a secluded room at Greystone, to talk about his father and the tournament that meant so much to him.

The first thing he did was compliment nearly every person who has contributed to the success of the Bruno's Memorial Classic. He listed so many names that I lost track.

Bruno said he didn't want any of the credit for the tournament's success or any attention. He was gracious and kind during the interview. But the look on his face and the tone of his voice kept telling me that he wasn't sure he was doing the right thing, talking about himself, talking about his family.

But a smile came to his face when he talked about his childhood ... and his father.

Bruno said every Sunday afternoon in the spring and summer, the two of them had a ritual. They watched professional golf on television.

"My father and I would sit in the living room and watch these guys playing golf," Bruno said. "He loved to watch it. Had he been here this week, he would spend most of his time in the players' lounge, talking and kidding with the guys."

Angelo Bruno also loved to play golf. Every Saturday, at noon, he had a regular game with Vince Saia, Anthony Ross, and Bill Owen at Inverness Country Club.

To say they had fun playing golf would be an understatement.

"He loved golf and this tournament was his dream," Saia said.

Saia and Bruno also were avid football fans. But despite the fact they had different allegiances—Saia to Auburn and Bruno to Alabama—they still attended the Iron Bowl together.

"Although we did take Father Brian Egan with us to all the games and let him sit in the middle," Saia said, smiling.

Like his father, Ronnie Bruno also plays golf. But he admits to having few skills (his handicap is 20) at the game. There are too many responsibilities now for the 40-year-old chairman of a $2.7 billion company, which operates grocery stores in five states, to have a perfect swing.

Of course, during this time, he has also played a role in running this golf tournament. Several weeks ago, he opened a temporary office at Greystone, where he ran not only the grocery store chain but also the golf tournament.

Perhaps when the tournament ends, he will be able to reflect on the events of the past few months and make some sense out of it all.

He probably needs to take a deep breath.

Three weeks before his father died, Ronnie and his wife, Lee Ann, had their first child, Ronald Gregory.

Then came the death of his father and Ronnie's ascension to the chairmanship of Bruno's, Inc.

"And two weeks after that," Bruno said, "I had my fortieth birthday.

Now, as I look back, it seems like a big blur."

Where he has found the strength to endure?

"Somehow, the Good Lord gives you strength for the times in need."

As he talked about his faith, the subject of stock car driver Clifford Allison's death came up. Earlier this week, on Tuesday, Bruno and Bobby Allison were visiting on hole No. 10 during the Shootout.

Two days later, Allison's son was dead.

"That's such a terrible tragedy," Bruno said.

"It's something you hope you never have to go through again, I know what they're going through."

That was all Ronnie Bruno could say. He had spoken about things dear to him, so near to him. Now, he was silent.

But the memory of his father's dream lives on. It was been shared this week at Greystone by thousands of people and it will continue through tomorrow night.

Angelo Bruno did not live to see the first Bruno's Memorial Classic. But what a wonderful legacy he left behind.

I was always particularly pleased with this column because of my strong fondness for the Bruno family. That first year, the winner of the golf tournament was secondary behind remembering the lives of Angelo and Lee Bruno.

SEPTEMBER 7, 1992

Cut "The Deuce" loose

David Palmer has to go. No debate. No discussion. Just get rid of him.

And do it now. Do it before he destroys the most talented team assembled at Alabama in more than a decade. Do it now before he humiliates Coach Gene Stallings any more than he already has done.

Do it now for the sanity of all Alabama fans, particularly those who cried out and supported him, who asked after his June arrest that he be given a fair shake.

In the wake of Palmer's June DUI arrest, Stallings had a difficult decision.

The best punishment, Stallings believed, would be to keep him out of the Vanderbilt game. It was a move widely praised, a move many people thought would help Palmer get back on the right track.

Well, that right track lasted approximately 12 hours. That, of course, ended when Palmer was picked up on U.S. Highway 11 by a state trooper and charged with driving under the influence.

"It made me sick to my stomach," Stallings said yesterday. "I don't know if we'll get it resolved or not."

What are Stallings's choices? Of course, he could do everything possible to help (which he should and probably will do anyway), and then let him earn his way back on the team. In other words, suspend him for a couple of games and if Palmer proves he is a good citizen, let him back on.

The other choice apparently would be to kick Palmer off the team for the rest of the year.

This is the right choice. If he fails to do this, Stallings destroys the well-earned reputation he has as a disciplinarian. By failing to throw him out, Stallings sends out the message to his team and to the rest of college football that winning is the only important thing at Alabama. Clearly, as important as Palmer is to the program, he cannot be above the program. Palmer needs help of some kind. I don't know whether or not he has a drinking problem or simply trouble dealing with reality. But his blatant disregard for his coach, the university and the law is unconscionable. Remember the stories a few weeks ago. Remember when Palmer talked about lessons learned. He spoke of remorse and regret.

Today, those are hollow words, indeed.

What is so tragic, so sad, is that a brilliant career could be going down the drain.

Palmer is no ordinary athlete.

"The Deuce" is one of the most talented athletes we have seen in the state. Perhaps Bo Jackson was a better runner. But don't tell me Bo sprinting for a touchdown was as exciting as when Palmer got loose on a punt return.

Everything was right there in front of him. Certainly, it is no secret he wasn't born with a silver spoon in his mouth. He came from a tough neighborhood. But Stallings has talked repeatedly of the improvement he's made since coming to Alabama.

He's grown up, Stallings said, You should have seen Palmer when he first got here, the coach often says.

Well, Coach, we're looking at him now. We're looking at a young man with the whole world in front of him, a good shot at the Heisman Trophy, who now has a deuce of his own: two DUIs on his record in less than three months.

He certainly leads the Southeastern Conference in that category.

Immediately, Alabama fans will begin to wonder what effect his departure might have on the season.

It will hurt if Stallings suspends him for the year. Alabama defeated Vanderbilt by 17 points on Saturday. But it had little spark offensively, the kind of excitement and flair the Tide enjoys when Palmer is in the lineup.

Will it cost Alabama a shot at the national championship or an SEC title?

Possibly.

While the Tide probably can survive the season better without Palmer than, say, Jay Barker, the young man made a difference. If you don't believe it, just ask Vanderbilt last year about the 56-yard punt return or Tulane about the one that went 69 yards.

Or check with the folks in Baton Rouge, Louisiana, about the 90-yard punt return that proved to be the difference or the 10-yard run against Auburn, which helped spell the measure between victory and defeat.

Yes, Palmer will be missed if Stallings suspends him.

But the point will be missed even more if he stays.

And the point is he was given a chance. It only took him until 2:30 a.m. yesterday to prove he was unworthy of another chance to be a member of this year's team.

A lot of Alabama fans are thankful Gene Stallings did not take my advice. Without Palmer, the Tide would not have won the national championship. Now, of course, that never entered Stallings's mind when making the decision.

SEPTEMBER 25, 1992

Majors should butt out

Apparently, Johnny Majors is familar with the story of Wally Pipp. And doesn't want a repeat of it.

Pipp, of course, was the starting first baseman for the New York Yankees who was injured in 1925 and replaced in the lineup by a young kid named Lou Gehrig. From that day on until 1939, Gehrig never missed a game on the road to immortality.

Pipp was never heard from again.

Sitting on a living room couch last Saturday, watching the Phil Fulmer-coached Tennessee Volunteers dismantle No. 4

Florida at fabled Neyland Stadium, Majors must have thought of that story. And suddenly, his health took a dramatic turn for the better.

Majors was well again, even though the 57-year-old had had heart bypass surgery less than a month earlier.

"You can only read so many books and watch so many movies," Majors said.

That is true. But that doesn't mean you have to mess up a good thing, which Majors has done by coming back.

But that is typical of Majors. This may sound harsh or insensitive. Especially for a man coming off a serious illness. But if Majors were a good soldier, one who really cared for his school instead of himself, he would have taken his time coming back.

Perhaps, even sit out the season.

Right now, Phil Fulmer is the most popular man in east Tennessee. And he has earned the applause with his brilliant coaching in recent weeks.

But Majors's ego, which at last check was the size of Jupiter, couldn't handle someone else's being successful with his program.

This is the reason for the sudden return.

This is not to say that Majors hasn't done a good job as the Tennessee skipper. But at 57, in questionable health, this would seem to be an opportune time for him to walk cautiously, perhaps even contemplate retirement.

Tennessee officials could have killed two birds with one stone by firing Doug Dickey, the school's cloddish athletic director, and replacing him with Majors. Then they could name Fulmer as the head coach.

If you don't think Fulmer has done the best coaching job in the nation this season, you haven't been paying very close attention.

But if history proves correct, Majors will find a way to blow this season. There is little doubt about his record against Tennessee's No. 1 opponent—Alabama.

Majors's record against Alabama is 4-11, including defeats in the last six games. In at least the last three games, Tennessee has had superior talent, but Majors has managed to find a way to lose. So he has returned. The fans in Knoxville are pleased that his health has improved. However, some are not overwhelmed he returned so quickly.

On the local talk shows in Knoxville, you can bet most of the conversation this week concerns the return of Majors.

"It's been an interesting week," said Mike Keith, the host of the show on WIVK radio, the flagship station of the Volunteers.

"Right now, I would say the calls are running about 50-50 on his return. Some people are saying if it's not broke, don't fix it. Others are saying he's been the head coach for 16 years and should do whatever he wants."

While Majors has certainly been a fixture at Tennessee for the last two decades, Keith correctly points out he is not regarded in the same light as some other long-standing coaches. In other words, he can't walk on water.

"John Majors is not exactly Bear Bryant," Keith said. "Not everyone has always loved him."

If for some reason Majors were to leave, would Fulmer be the choice?

"He would be overwhelming," said Keith.

John Adams, the sports editor of the *Knoxville News-Sentinel*, agreed.

"I think they would storm the building if Fulmer didn't get the job."

And rightfully so.

Majors blew it by letting his ego get in the way with his shocking return. He couldn't stand to see someone else do well.

Of course, Majors could rectify the situation by stepping down.

We all know he won't do it. But it would be the right thing to do, for himself and the Tennessee program.

This column, which was picked up and run in the Knoxville newspaper, is credited by some as being a catalyst in the demise of Majors at Tennessee. For that, I feel as if I have made a lasting benefaction to my alma mater.

OCTOBER 5, 1992

Dear Mr. Kramer: Get rid of South Carolina

Commissioner Roy Kramer
Southeastern Conference Office
2201 Civic Center Blvd.
Birmingham, AL 35203

Dear Mr. Commissioner:

Sorry to bother you. I know you are a busy man and out of town a great deal. My sources tell me you have just returned from Arkansas State and TCU to discuss the prospects of adding those two fine insititutions to the league. After all, you have to have parity.

I have just returned home from one of the most miserable afternoons of my sportswriting career. I have driven through a driving rainstorm from Tuscaloosa, where I believe I witnessed the most repugnant football team in the storied history of the SEC.

When you hand out awards next spring in Destin, Florida, at the annual meeting, you should give Alabama Coach Gene Stallings the "Man of the Year" Award for the kindness and generosity he displayed in not leaving his first team in and going for the all-time scoring record set by Georgia Tech in a 222-0 victory over Cumberland.

It would not have been difficult. Nothing is difficult when you are playing South Carolina. That is, except taking the Gamecocks seriously.

So, Commissioner, do us all a favor and call an emergency meeting of the league's executive committee and, in the best interest of the SEC, throw the Gamecocks out of the league.

Of course, there is something positive to say about the South Carolina defense. It made Alabama's offense look good.

Stallings even sent quarterback Brian Burgdorf into the game. The youngster put in a creditable performance.

Although South Carolina is at the top of my gripe list, there are some other problems in this league.

While your spin doctors try to talk about this being the best football league in the nation, I urge you to think again.

I do not think I have ever seen more pitiful football than what has been displayed this fall in the mighty SEC.

First of all, take Arkansas ... please.

You have put this television package together with Jefferson-Pilot. I understand the agreement calls for every school to be shown at least once.

I have no argument with Saturday's Arkansas-Georgia game. Tennessee-LSU was taken by ESPN, so your choices were down to some barf-bag specials: Ole Miss-Kentucky, South Carolina-Alabama, and Georgia-Arkansas.

I figured you did not show what shaped up as the best game of the day—Auburn-Vanderbilt—because you were saving the Tigers for Saturday's encounter with Mississippi State.

But my friendly *TV Guide* shows that next week's schedule calls for the Arkansas-Tennessee game to be televised. What a joke!

The Auburn-Mississippi State game shapes up as one of the most important battles of the year in the Western Division.

ESPN cannot show the game in prime time because it already has committed to a Notre Dame-Pittsburgh game that features teams that lost Saturday to Stanford and Maryland, (dis) respectively.

I don't know anything about oddsmaking, but I'm sure Tennessee will be favored in this game by only 30 or 40 points.

Of course, there are some other wonderful teams in your league this year, such as LSU, a loser to Colorado State (and everyone else).

Incredibly, such schools as Kentucky, Vanderbilt, and Ole Miss now are respectable, thanks to the addition of South Carolina and Arkansas and the decline of LSU.

Commissioner, what I propose to you is simple. If you want to keep Arkansas and South Carolina, fine. You got to dance with those who brung you (down).

But I suggest you hop on an airplane right now and get out to Texas A&M and Oklahoma and start doing some quick stepping.

Losing Florida State to the Atlantic Coast Conference was a major blunder. Getting South Carolina instead was even worse.

That's like being dumped by Julia Roberts and marrying Roseanne Barr.

It is time to stop the hemorrhaging. Do something before it is too late.

This is a great football conference. And I think the SEC title game on December 5 will be the talk of the nation.

But so will sludge such as Arkansas and South Carolina if you do not do something to correct it.

Sincerely,

Your Pal Paul

This column made me a persona non grata in South Carolina. When I visited Columbia a year later, there were banners about me and buttons being passed out, which read "Kill Finebaum." Fortunately, I survived the evening. Unfortunately, South Carolina remains a member of the SEC.

NOVEMBER 23, 1992

Dye controversy is coming to a head

AUBURN—He lingered, as if there were nowhere else to go. He talked and listened and talked some more.

Outside, on this late November day, the sky was gray and the wind was howling in the distance.

Perhaps this was why Patrick Fain Dye, now in the autumn of his career, hung around roughly 25 minutes after his news conference, chatting with a couple of reporters.

The conversation was pedestrian. But Dye was enjoying it, as if he were savoring the moment.

These are troubled times for Auburn's head football coach. A brilliant coaching career has been torched by an ex-football player/mercenary, his gold-digging wife and a headline-seeking attorney.

Yet, for all the adjectives about Mr. and Mrs. Eric Ramsey and their mouthpiece, Donald Watkins, the troika—better known as Team Ramsey—is far ahead of Dye in the fourth quarter of the biggest game of his storied career.

So perhaps for those reasons Dye was taking his time this morning. He, better than anyone, probably was aware his next trip to this media room could be his last.

Finally, as the room emptied, he turned to me and said: "Where you going?"

This was Dye's way of inviting me to lunch.

However, lunch at Sewell Hall did not interest me on this day. I was more interested in visiting privately with Dye instead of competing for his attention between bites of fried okra and black-eyed peas.

I've known Dye a long time. I first covered him when I was the Auburn beat reporter for the *Birmingham Post-Herald*. We have sparred often in the past. I probably have brutalized Dye harder in print than any other person in the state—including Bill Curry.

But I've always liked him and respected him and—yes—even admired him.

Unlike so many of the phonies in today's coaching world, Dye is a straight shooter. He understands my business and respects it.

"You just wanted to see I was still alive, didn't you?" Dye was saying now as we climbed the stairwell and walked past closed doors and empty offices.

It had been awhile since Dye and I had spoken to one another with any degree of substance. After a column last summer about his health and future, several members of Dye's immediate family had called and complained. Since then, the relationship between us had been strained.

"I don't think anybody is here," Dye said.

It was quiet. There wasn't a soul to be found.

We entered Dye's spacious office and he motioned me to sit in a chair at his round, circular glass desk.

"I just wanted to see how you were, ask a couple of questions about your future and the NCAA case and your relationship with Dr. Muse," I said.

Dye shot a look at me as if I had just pulled a gun on him.

"Can you talk about it?" I asked.

"Hell, no," Dye replied.

Honestly, I really didn't care if Dye would publicly discuss the Ramsey case or not. I wanted this visit for sentimental reasons. I thought it might be our last while he served as Auburn's head coach.

Dye offered me a pastry brought to him the day before by a loyal Auburn fan from Birmingham. We both munched and the conversation continued.

Although I have heard and read Dye's protests about resigning, I have tried to watch this soap opera without rose-colored glasses. Based partly on Auburn president William Muse's reactions the day of the NCAA letter, and conventional wisdom, it has been my conclusion that Thursday's game with Alabama will be Dye's last at Auburn.

I told Dye I understood he had to maintain his position of refusing to resign. But was it really true?

"I have no intention of resigning," Dye said emphatically.

But you must think about it at times?

"I coach every day like I'm going to be here forever," Dye said. "And I coach every day like it's going to be my last."

But will it be? That is the question Auburn fans are asking these days. While everyone seems to have an opinion, no one is really certain of the future—including Dye.

Clearly, he is not ready to go gently into the night. Apparently, university officials also are willing to let this drama play out a little longer.

Although the rumor mill is ripe with stories of buyouts and coaching candidates being contacted, the official Auburn position is that the school will proceed with Dye for the time being.

Although Muse's statements three weeks ago seemed to indicate Dye's days were numbered, most insiders maintain he really had no choice in his stoic, hardline position.

"I can't believe he got up there and said all that crap," one person inside the Auburn athletic complex said of Muse. "He should have defended Coach Dye."

But Dye said he understood.

"I have a great relationship with Dr. Muse, I have no problems with anything he said."

Some Auburn people believe Muse was more upset with Dye's comments to *The Huntsville Times* than anything else. In that interview, Dye admitted Auburn had broken some NCAA rules.

Dye maintains the interview was intended to be off-the-record. However, the man who conducted the interview, John Pruett, is one of the most respected sportswriters in the state. Even some close associates of Dye's believe Pruett acted properly in his reporting of the story.

Although some Auburn fans want Dye out, it is known he (and Muse) are getting volumes of mail supporting his cause.

On Dye's desk was a stack of unopened letters. He read a couple as we talked.

There also is support in *The Plainsman*, the Auburn student paper. Last Thursday, a letter from student Donnie Peek said:

"What's wrong with you hypocritical hillbillies? If he (Dye) leaves, it will be the worst thing to happen to Auburn since the Doug Barfield era. I would rather go through three years of probation and have a coach I respect than bow to bureaucratic witch hunters. If Dye leaves, it will be a long time before I go to another Auburn game."

It is unclear whether or not Auburn would receive a harsher penalty if Dye remains—but it's possible.

So the school is faced with an uncomfortable situation. Should it cut its losses by forcing Dye out? Or should it keep him?

Firing him at the moment seems out of the question.

Although there are clauses in Dye's contract that state the school can fire him if he violates NCAA rules, you almost could bet the coach would sue the university if he were dismissed outright.

Dye is believed to have a five-year rollover contract, which pays him a base salary of approximately $150,000. Officials estimate Dye's entire package (including shoe contracts, television, endorsements, etc.) is roughly $550,000.

In addition to NCAA sanctions, would Auburn want to fight its most successful head football coach in court?

Or would it be better for the school to attempt to buy him out and allow him to resign gracefully?

It is a possibility. But it would be expensive.

Muse must walk a careful line in these proceedings. While he wants to do the right thing in the eyes of the NCAA, he also must be concerned about the constituency that pays his salary.

If he blows Dye out and brings in a coach who fails, the next firing at Auburn might be his own (see Joab Thomas).

Supporters of the embattled coach are concerned that Muse really doesn't understand that Dye mystique.

Muse wasn't around in 1981, when Dye took over a program in shambles. Muse wasn't around to witness an Auburn program rising from the ashes to become one of the most feared in the nation. Instead of Sugar Bowl trips and Heisman Trophy winners, Muse arrived to see a program in turmoil. Although the Auburn spirit is wounded, at least there is some.

That was not the case when Dye arrived.

Athletic director Mike Lude perhaps has a better appreciation of what Dye has accomplished. But Lude is not expected to be the key decision-maker in this.

If Auburn does nothing, the school walks a dangerous line, risking damage to another recruiting season. It is unlikely the school's problems with NCAA will be resolved until April, long after recruiting ends.

But even if Dye were dismissed next week, how much could a new coach do for the time being? There still would be the NCAA cloud hanging over the program. Unless the program hired a coach with incredible credentials and charisma, this year's recruiting would be very difficult.

Although Dye's health often is talked about, it is unlikely this problem will be a critical issue in determining his short-term future.

Would a victory Thursday influence the decision?

Some people maintain it might give Dye a way to go out on a high note. However, it might strengthen his position with the school, thus helping his cause.

Although this has been a disappointing season, Dye is optimistic about next year. He would have a more experienced offense, a senior quarterback he has confidence in and running back Steve Davis, the top high school player in the nation last fall.

Still, most Auburn people think the bottom line is the NCAA. If Dye's role in the Ramsey case can be minimized, one would think his chances of survival would be helped.

"That's the shame of this whole thing," said one person who is very close to Dye. "For someone like Eric Ramsey to ruin a great man's career like his would be a tragedy. Pat Dye is not a cheater. Here is a person with as little character as Ramsey, who begged and pleaded for money from anyone he ever met, dismantling this man's wonderful career. If he gets away with it, that would be a tragedy for the human race."

The hour with Dye had passed quickly. Outside, the weather remained dark and gloomy, much like the mood inside the athletic complex.

"I got to get out of here," Dye said, standing up from behind his desk. "I got to get out to the country."

There, he will clear his head and think about an uncertain future. There, he will ponder the Alabama game, always an important game. This year, it could be his last.

As we walked out of Dye's office, he put his arm around me, like a father puts his arm around a son.

"I just want you to know that nothing has changed between us, no matter what you write or say."

With that, Dye closed his office door. It was quiet now. The athletic complex remained empty, and the only sound came from the howling wind outside.

Two days after this column appeared, Dye announced his resignation as Auburn's coach. He probably figured if I was going to start writing nice stories about him, perhaps it was time to get out.

DECEMBER 14, 1992

10 years later, it's Stallings

It was 8:30 p.m. when the phone rang. A loud, shrill ring.

At first, I ignored it. I was taking a couple of days off from work and really wasn't in the mood to talk to anyone.

Finally, 10 years ago today, I answered it on the fourth ring. My boss was calling. The conversation was short. But he had said a mouthful.

"Some guy form California called and said he heard a crazy rumor that Bear Bryant was resigning."

"Are you kidding?"

I didn't wait for a response. I grabbed my coat and headed downtown.

The next three hours were as chaotic as any I've ever encountered in my career. The phone kept ringing and the story kept changing. Was it true or just another hoax?

Finally, as the night wore on, the newswires picked up on the story. Herschel Nissenson of The Associated Press was quoting sources saying Bryant was resigning and Ray Perkins would be taking his place. United Press International and *The Washington Post* had a different story.

Their dispatches said Bryant was only going to announce he would be stepping down in a year and that Perkins would come in to serve as offensive coordinator.

In the midst of it all, I got a call from the sports editor of *The New York Times.* I told him we had checked it out and believed the rumors to be true.

He laughed at me.

The sports editor of the almighty *New York Times* told me "there was no way the coach of the New York Giants was leaving to take over at Alabama."

But about 11 p.m., the story began to take shape. That was, until I reached Bryant's home and talked to Mary Harmon.

She said Coach Bryant was out recruiting. Someone else got hold of Bryant's daughter, and she said, "This story is not what you people think it is."

Finally, about 11:30 p.m., someone at the newspaper had come up with Perkins's home number in New Jersey. Did I care that it was 12:30 a.m. on the East Coast? Not on your life.

Carolyn Perkins answered and told me her husband was in bed and could not be disturbed. When I told her the story, she paused and offered no comment.

Of course, early the next morning, in Tuscaloosa, Bryant announced he was resigning, admitting he was just "a tired old man" in a young man's game.

"There comes a time when you need to hang it up," the 69-year-old coach, clad in crimson jacket and reading from a prepared statement, said in a sad, low voice. "And that time has come for me as head football coach at the University of Alabama."

Dr. Joab Thomas, the university president, sat to Bryant's right watching solemnly as the coach finished the emotional address.

Finally, when Bryant sat down, Thomas announced that Perkins had signed a five-year contract, but few seemed interested in that.

There was sadness everywhere in the athletic department. As I walked around, looking for reactions from coaches and staff, the sound of sniffling and sobbing could be heard throughout the building.

I'll never forget walking into Mal Moore's office. Moore was the offensive coordinator and a man who had desperately wanted the job.

"I have no comment," he said firmly. "Would you just let me off the hook with that?"

The next day, I called Perkins in New Jersey.

I asked his secretary if I might get an appointment with him sometime over the weekend.

However, before I could finish, Perkins had picked up the phone.

"Why don't we talk right now," said Perkins, never a man to waste time. And we did for almost 45 minutes. Perkins sounded like a kid in a candy store.

A few minutes later, I placed another call. This one was to Irving, Texas, to the headquarters of the Dallas Cowboys.

But the tone of this conversation was dramatically different. The fellow at the other end spoke softly. There was deep hurt in his voice.

The coach said he had wanted the Alabama job. Thought he had it.

He chose his words carefully, but the inference was clear to me. The man at the other end felt strongly that Bryant had wanted him as his successor.

Although he lost out on the opportunity of a lifetime, the coach said he was not going to wallow in the disappointment. The man said life goes on. He said you have to look forward and not dwell on what might have been.

Finally, he thanked me for calling. Then, Gene Stallings said good-bye.

Two weeks after this column, Gene Stallings was carried off the field, the toast of college football.

December 19, 1992

Lude's hiring a bust?

When Auburn hired Mike Lude last spring to replace Pat Dye as athletic director, the 69-year-old administrator was hailed as one of the finest in the business.

"He's got to be one of the most qualified athletic directors in the country," said Don James, the highly respected Washington coach.

Dr. William Muse, the Auburn president, was also overjoyed with his first major athletic hiring, luring Lude from the Blockbuster Bowl, where he served as executive director.

"Auburn University has put together its own 'Blockbuster' deal," Muse said.

However, in his short tenure on the Plains, Lude has hardly been a blockbuster.

Perhaps, a better choice of words might be a bust.

Some Auburn faithful are now privately wondering if Dr. Muse shouldn't begin to consider the possibility of cutting Lude loose.

"He has to go before he destroys Auburn," said one influential Auburn booster, who asked not be identified.

Apparently, there are a number of Auburn faithful who see it the same way.

Lude's handling of the Auburn coaching search was a complete embarrassment to the school and its alumni, according to several highly placed observers.

"If one didn't know any better, you would have thought Joab Thomas was advising Lude on the coaching search," said one person.

Actually, according to several officials, all of who requested anonymity, Lude seemed to follow Thomas's thinking in at least one aspect.

According to these people, Lude's first choice for the Auburn job was Clemson coach Ken Hatfield. Thomas, the former Alabama president, called Hatfield after Ray Perkins resigned. However, Hatfield turned down the opportunity to be interviewed.

Of course, Thomas then settled on Bill Curry.

"That's who he tried to push down the committee," one person said of Lude. "It was Ken Hatfield."

On Thursday, Lude denied he had ever contacted Hatfield about the job.

"Absolutely not," Lude said. "Of course, Ken is a very close friend of mine. Now he did write me a personal note but not about the Auburn situation."

At the new conference Thursday, the subject of Lude's performance was raised in a question to Muse.

When a reporter said to Muse that some people "felt Mike Lude bungled the process," Muse replied:

"We are very satisfied with the results."

It appeared to several in the audience that Muse was evading the question.

When pressed further on the subject and asked if he remained supportive of Lude, Muse responded:

"Certainly."

But that was it. And some people interpreted the remark as less than a ringing endorsement of Auburn's athletic director.

So where did Lude go wrong?

First of all, officials close to the situation blame Lude for much of the constant stream of misinformation in the media, which caused Auburn untold embarrassment during this process. This was not what Dr. Muse or anyone at Auburn expected last spring, when Lude was hired at a salary of $150,000 a year, including a $30,000 housing allowance.

It is believed the average athletic director at major schools in the conference—including Alabama—makes between $100,000 and $115,000 a year.

"He sold Muse on the fact that he could wave a magic wand and make everything right," and one person close to the situation. "He sold him on the fact that he had excellent contacts with the NCAA. What he sold him was a bill of goods." Lude coached football for 23 years before becoming an athletic director at Kent State in 1970. He spent 16 years at Washington before he resigned to become executive director at the Blockbuster Bowl. It is widely believed he was forced out of Washington after a dispute with the administration.

Still, he is an articulate communicator and has a strong reputation.

"He reminds me a lot of Bill Curry," said one person who has worked with Lude on occasion. "Lude is also not short on ego. He's also a name-dropper. If you listen to him long enough, every coach in football is one of his closest friends." When Dye announced his resignation, it was widely felt Lude would use those contacts to draw a big-name coach to Auburn. Some speculated it might be James, his former friend and associate at Washington.

"Auburn University has the prestige and tradition to attract an established head coach," Lude said. "We're not looking for on-the-job training."

Almost immediately, according to sources, Lude went to people such as Hatfield and Fisher DeBerry, the Air Force coach.

Of course, Lude did not follow the normal practices, such as informally feeling coaches out. Instead, according to his critics, Lude directly contacted athletic directors at the schools of the head coaches, which led to a rash of news stories.

"It began to look like another Joab Thomas railroad job," said one person close to the situation.

It is believed Lude tried to push Hatfield on the committee. However, the committee is thought to have informed Lude it was not interested in the Clemson coach. The committee would eventually interview seven people. They were Sheridan, Auburn defensive coordinator Wayne Hall, TCU coach Pat Sullivan, Southern Cal coach Larry Smith, Georgia Tech coach Bill Lewis, Georgia Southern coach Tim Stowers, and Terry Bowden of Samford.

At first, there did not seem to be consensus. Several members of the committee seemed to favor Hall. A few others were high on Sullivan.

But Muse and Lude—who did not have a vote—expressed concern over Hall and Sullivan. Since the committee had agreed the choice would be unanimous, the favorites of the Auburn faithful were dead.

Bowden seemed to emerge as a compromise choice of the Hall and Sullivan supporters, and the rest went along.

But what about Miami Coach Dennis Erickson?

It is felt that a lot of the Erickson talk came as a result of Lude's relationship with the Miami coach. Some felt Lude kept floating Erickson's name, which confused the issue. Perhaps, Lude's critics pointed out, he hoped things would become so confusing that he could slip one of his choices in the back door.

But it didn't work out that way.

After a weekend of interviewing, Bowden seemed to emerge by late Monday as the man.

However, it is believed, for unknown reasons, that Muse and Lude wanted to wait a couple of days to make the announcement public.

"I think Muse got this confused with a search for the chairman of the history department and didn't see the need for speed," said one person close to the situation. "He and Lude just didn't understand the environment down here."

It is believed Lude wanted time to inform the coaches who lost out to give them time to officially withdraw from contention in order to save face.

For instance, DeBerry pulled out Tuesday night, and he was never even interviewed. The same day, Erickson again denied his interest. On Wednesday, Sullivan, Sheridan, and Lewis withdrew their names from contention.

In the process, Auburn was embarrassed and humiliated by the news stories, which seemed to indicate that nobody wanted the job.

The person several prominent Auburn officials and supporters blame for this is Lude.

"Mike Lude completely screwed up this entire process," said one official. "This entire mess is his fault."

So will Lude survive?

That is a tough question to answer. When he was hired, Lude promised to stay at Auburn for no more than two years.

Six months of that time are now down the drain. Some Auburn faithful are concerned the school's athletic department will follow suit if Lude is allowed to remain in charge much longer.

After this column appeared, some insiders feeling Lude had been severly damaged, predicted he wouldn't last the month as Auburn's athletic director. Lude retired as Auburn's athletic director in April 1994.

DECEMBER 31, 1992

Miami's vile talk disgusts

NEW ORLEANS—The word "dynasty" often is used to describe the accomplishments of the University of Miami football team. And with very good reason.

A victory tomorrow night over Alabama would give the school five national championships in 10 years. By now, of course, you should know all of this by heart.

However, usually when people think of dynasties in college football, another word is often used: "Class."

Coach Paul "Bear" Bryant preached it every day of his career. It was the hallmark of his great teams. Bryant wanted his players to show their class and be good citizens. At times, it sounded hokey. But there was substance behind the message.

But the word class is never used to describe Miami. Perhaps a more appropriate description is trash.

The Miami president, athletic director, and head football coach continually talk about cleaning up the red-light-district reputation of their program.

But talk is cheap.

Just hang around these guys for 10 minutes and you feel violated. Yesterday, following a Miami press briefing, I wanted to immediately run upstairs and shower. I wanted to wash away the sleaze and slime that might have stuck to me after getting close to these guys.

Perhaps it is unfair to characterize an entire program this way. Some Miami people are good folks.

But the ones I've encountered so far are vile and disgusting.

Regardless of Miami's success in the polls, this program is giving the good name of college football a black eye.

The stories about Miami players having brushes with the law are legendary. The joke used to be that the Hurricanes were No. 1 in the AP, CNN, UPI, and the FBI.

Take Rohan Marley ... please.

This guy is an All-American sleazebag.

"I like Bob Marley," Alabama running back Derrick Lassic said. "But I can't say the same for his son."

The son of the late reggae singer from Jamaica described Alabama's offense this way:

"They have no passing game. And one-dimensional teams are not complete teams. It's going to be a good night for us."

They call this "trash talk."

It happens on football fields every Saturday in the fall. But nowhere is it louder and nastier and more defiled than in Miami.

One of the ringleaders of the "Trash Brigade" is Michael Barrow, a 6-foot-2 senior linebacker who earned first-team All-America honors and was a Butkus Award finalist.

Yesterday, Barrow spoke at length about the trash talking that has become as much a trademark as the "U" on their helmets.

Barrow, of all things, accused Alabama's Antonio Langham of firing the first bash in the battle of trash.

After quarterback Gino Torretta won the Heisman Trophy, Langham said he would like to be able to intercept the highly honored quarterback and run one back for a touchdown.

"That set the tone," Barrow said.

"Alabama started talking like they had already had their ring sizes made. They were overlooking us and we didn't appreciate it. When somebody starts talking about one of the family, we pull together."

Of all my years of covering football—sans the Bill Curry era— I'm not sure I've heard more hogwash than was spewing out of this guy's mouth.

"Hey, man," Barrow continued. "We're Miami. You don't talk like that about us."

Barrow was asked if Langham and Alabama would be punished for their actions. In other words, for having the nerve to speak ill of Miami.

"I wouldn't say punish," Barrow said smirking, giving the impression of a gang leader in Liberty City, Florida, trying to decide the proper punishment to be handed out to a captured enemy. "But if you're going to talk the talk, you'd better be able to walk the walk."

A few minutes later, Tide linebacker Antonio London showed up in the same room. He shook his head upon hearing Barrow's trash.

"Miami fired the first shot," London said. "When we got the bowl bid, they were the ones who were saying, 'What's Alabama doing here? They don't deserve it.' "

Of course, trash talk is not going away at Miami.

"Whoever the coach is," Barrow said, "he'd better get used to it. Coach E. [Erickson] did. You learn this from the hood. You could bring the Pope in here to coach and he would end up doing it. It's part of Miami talking trash and doing it in style."

Pope John Paul II was unavailable for comment yesterday, so we don't know what the pontiff thinks about the trash talk.

But one thing is certain. What might be style to Michael Barrow and his gang stinks to any decent human being.

Miami might be the top program in all of college football. The Hurricanes might have the records to back it up.

However, all the glitter and gold of their national championship trophies won't remove the stench from this program. The Miami football program is bush-league.

And that's no trash talk.

After writing this column, I became more and more convinced that Alabama would pull the Miami upset.

JANUARY 2, 1993

Tradition topples the trash

NEW ORLEANS—In a century of championship football at the University of Alabama, there have been some monumental victories.

Remember the Rose Bowl team and the famed goal-line stand against Penn State?

Oh, there are so many to remember, so many to treasure and reflect on.

But, my friends, shoot the 1993 Sugar Bowl to the top of the list.

This 34-13 victory over Miami, for the national championship, is one for the ages.

This time, the Tide didn't need the heroics of Antonio Langham.

Instead, Alabama's national championship was won with monumental plays the entire game, especially an epic explosion in the third quarter that might go down as one of the greatest in the Tide's storied history.

Someone said later that the outburst against the Hurricanes came in waves, like say, a Crimson Tide.

This wasn't just a win over the most feared school in college football. The Tide dismantled the Hurricanes, breaking Miami's 29-game winning streak and shattering the 'Canes bid to take a place as one of the great dynasties in college football.

For weeks, the Miami players have trashed the Alabama program. They talked of Alabama being a one-dimensional team. They insinuated the Tide had no business playing in a game of this magnitude.

As ridiculous as that talk sounded to folks in Alabama, interestingly, most of the national media seemed to agree.

But, somehow, this Alabama team reached down and did pull off the upset.

The Tide did its talking on the field. There was nothing trashy about it. It was a wonderful display of old-fashioned, hard-nosed, smash-mouth football.

Sitting in the Superdome last night, watching the incredible celebration below, it was hard to believe how far this program has come in such a short time.

From an 0-3 start to the Gene Stallings era to a national championship. Three years was all it took.

Clearly, Alabama will be back next season as one of the teams to beat along with Florida State.

Something tells me the thrashing of Miami might make pollsters slightly hesitant to rank the Hurricanes at the top of the heap again next season.

And now that Stallings has assured Alabama fans he has no interest in retirement, one can expect future good Tidings.

The job Stallings and his coaching staff did this season was unbelievable.

Although Stallings never said so publicly, he was personally troubled by the trash talk from the Miami players.

While they chirped all week, he kept his team's eyes quietly focused on the prize. Alabama players hardly left their hotel.

He hoped his players would not be intimidated by the talk. Instead, it seemed to motivate the Tide.

While mistakes were made during the first half, primarily with turnovers, one could tell the Tide was on a roll.

Had it not been for some incredibly bad calls by the crew from the Southwest Conference, the Tide might have put the game out of reach during the first 30 minutes.

And in the third quarter, Alabama came through, blowing a hole in the Miami game plan the size of the eye of a hurricane.

There was a flickering moment late in the game when Miami narrowed the gap to 27-13. But once again, Derrick Lassic answered the call, making some in the audience last night wonder if the wrong man on the field had won the Heisman.

Well, Gino Torretta might have the Heisman Trophy. But Lassic and his teammates will have the rings.

They should fit very nicely.

Lassic simply was incredible last night, busting loose for 135 yards and two touchdowns. The antithesis was true of Torretta, who completed 24 of 56 passes and was haunted all night by a Tide defense that should go down as one of the greatest in college football history.

Toward the end of the game, ABC sportscaster Keith Jackson said, "I feel sympathy" for him.

Well, that is absurd. I find it hard to feel sorry for anyone connected to Miami. It would be appropriate to say the devil finally got its due.

So did Jay Barker.

The young quarterback's statistics (4 of 13 with two interceptions) were abysmal. He gained more yards rushing (19) than he did passing (18).

You won't find that very often by quarterbacks in national championship encounters.

But you can't knock the kid's record as a starter (17-0) or his remarkable character.

So much now for talk of Alabama's soft schedule. A 13-0 record should put that to rest.

Of course, some Florida State fans probably will boast of having the best team in the nation. But as Miami found out last night, talk, particularly coming from the Sunshine State, can be rather cheap.

All that matters now is that Alabama is No. 1 in the land. It does have a familiar ring.

With all of the celebration and noise, one couldn't help but feel especially pleased for Stallings, his family, and especially, his son, John Mark.

As the game neared its conclusion ABC zeroed in on John Mark, who sat by his mother in a private box, overlooking the field.

The young man has had to overcome so much in his life. But, last night, thankfully, he was able to witness his dear "Papa" climb college football's highest mountain.

This was one of those special nights in sportswriting, covering an event of this magnitude.

JANUARY 4, 1993

After breaking from storied past, it's high Tide again

From 0-3 to 13-0.

From losing 35-0 to Florida to winning 34-13 over Miami.

From national chumps to national champs.

Such is the story of the University of Alabama's magnificent journey to the national championship.

It has been an endearing odyssey of sadness and joy, of heartbreaking scenes and heartfelt moments.

In a little more than 1,000 days, Alabama fans have witnessed everything from one of the most acrimonious coaching separations in school history, to one of the most exhilarating moments in a century of championship football.

Alabama's Sugar Bowl victory over Miami will be remembered for many things. But perhaps most noticable was how easy it seemed to be accomplished.

Somewhere up in Kentucky, among the resonance of bouncing basketballs on the hardwood, perhaps Bill Curry can be heard telling the story of this team. Let him talk the talk.

The rest doesn't even need to be said.

Finally, this decade-long odyssey in the wilderness, one that has been painful and debilitating to the Tide pride, has ended.

Alabama finally has found its present. Perhaps now, as a writer from the Associated Press said the other day, "Maybe now when greatness and 'Bama football are mentioned in the same sentence, it won't always be in the past tense."

Gene Stallings has never tried to patronize Bear Bryant as Curry shamelessly did.

Instead, Stallings has always displayed a genuine love and respect for Bryant. He has never seemed bothered or uncomfortable with the long, seemingly suffocating shadow that Bryant's memory has cast.

It is unfortunate that a great magazine such as *Sports Illustrated* rushed into print two weeks ago with its ridiculous tribute to Arthur Ashe as its 1992 "Sportsman of the Year." A more appropriate and fitting recipient would have been Eugene "Bebes" Stallings.

Alabama now has won 12 national championships in a century of football. However, this one might have been the most significant.

Fans in Alabama understand the school's football tradition. However, few people outside the state either knew—or wanted to acknowledge—there was an Alabama football program before Mama called Bryant home.

Alabama won a bushel full of national championships before Bryant arrived on the scene. Now, finally, a seemingly endless decade after his death, the Tide is high again.

This is what Curry and his brotherhood of the miserable still don't understand: Alabama is bigger than one man.

Alabama will always attract great athletes because of what it is and what it stands for. In no way is this meant to take anything away from Stallings. He, along with his staff, did a brilliant job this season.

It is hard to remember a staff ever doing a better job. However, these people won in part because they understood and used Alabama's tradition to their advantage, instead of abusing it the way Curry did.

However, this journey has been anything but easy. It also is worth remembering two other men who should share in the championship.

Many people thought school president Roger Sayers and athletic director Hootie Ingram were crazy when they gambled on Stallings, who had been fired twice and possessed a losing record.

Perhaps these two men knew what they were doing.

Alabama fans also deserve some credit. In my career of covering football, I don't believe I've seen or heard a louder, more enthusiastic supporting cast than the fans who showed up wearing crimson Friday night at the Superdome.

Many people thought Miami would thrive on the noise from the Alabama followers. Instead, the Hurricanes seemed to die with the noise from Alabama fans.

Even while the national press was force-feeding the nation buckets full of propaganda about Miami, Tide fans in New Orleans were predicting an Alabama victory.

In the process of winning the national championship, Alabama shattered a million myths. One was that a Southeastern Conference team couldn't win the national championship with an eight-game conference schedule (plus the title game). The second myth was that Miami was invincible.

People believed this hype about Miami tradition, about the Hurricanes being destiny's darling.

Of course, even after the game, some members of Miami's "Trash Brigade" were still running their motor mouths, probably, between dressing their cuts and applying ice to their battered and bruised bodies.

"If we played like we should've," All-America linebacker Michael Barrow said, "we would've kicked their butt."

But on Friday night, Miami was outplayed, outcoached, outprepared, outrun, and outclassed by Alabama.

Perhaps that is why the final act of Alabama's championship season was so sweet and so satisfying.

After some sleep, I wrote this column for the next day's newspaper. Naturally, I found some way to blast Bill Curry, which made me feel much better.

April 21, 1993

Tears of a clown: Quit crying, Dennis

Coach Dennis Erickson
Head Football Coach
University of Miami
P. O. Box 248167
Coral Gables, Fla. 33124

Dear Dennis:

Sorry to bother you during this period of mourning. But I caught a recent article in the Fort Lauderdale *Sun-Sentinel* where you were popping off about a number of issues. You were quoted as saying "I'm not over it," referring to your team's 34-13 loss to Alabama in the Sugar Bowl.

Considering what a lousy job you did preparing your team before the game and the even worse job of maintaining control during the game, that really isn't difficult to understand.

I also was amused to read in the article that you would like another shot at Alabama. You said the goal at Miami was to win the national championship, but, "I'm not sure our ultimate goal isn't to get an opportunity to play Alabama again ... . I would like to have one more chance to play them before I die. Heck, I'd play them in Tuscaloosa if they wanted." Dennis, I'm not a psychologist. Yet it seems you are having difficulty distinguishing between fantasy and reality.

In your fantasies, you might want to compete with Alabama one more time. But here in the real world, I would take a powder. You've already gotten your tail kicked once. Why not leave well enough alone?

However, that is not the reason for the missive.

In the interview, you mentioned how the bitterness of the loss was compounded when you were hit after the game by a cup of ice, which, you say, was thrown by an Alabama fan. I'm sure you have proof of that.

You also accuse an Alabama fan of roughing up your 13-year-old son. Again, I am certain you can back that up with evidence.

You go on to say you have been bombarded with abusive mail from Alabama since the Sugar Bowl.

I'm sorry, Dennis. But I don't believe any of these charges. I think you made them up because you're a big sore loser. A crybaby.

Why would Alabama fans want to abuse you, your son, your mailbox? After all, Alabama's victory over Miami was perhaps the greatest victory in school history.

It wasn't as if the game were decided on the last play or on a controversial call that sent the fans out of the stadium in a foul mood. Alabama whipped Miami so badly, the game was over at halftime.

Yet you told the *Sun-Sentinel*: "I don't think I've ever dealt with fans as abusive as Alabama's."

Hey, Dennis, have you ever taken a look at Miami's fans? In Webster's right next to the definition of "scumbag," there is a picture of a Hurricanes fan.

They are some of the most offensive and disgusting people I've ever encountered. Of course, they all hail from the lovely little banana republic in Dade County. So what would you expect?

Do I even need to remind you of the classless, vulgar behavior of your players in the days leading up to the game? (You probably were too busy working on that brilliant offensive plan to notice. You remember: Torretta to Teague for a touchdown.) Do I need to remind you that your players refused to shake hands with Alabama players before the game? Do I need to remind you of your star linebacker, Rohan Marley? In the French Quarter in the days leading up to the game, did you hear about the Jamaican Jerk shouting down some of the Alabama players?

"You must be an offensive lineman, you fat, sloppy ...," he said to Alabama's Roosevelt Patterson.

Dennis, I suppose you taught your players how to behave in public.

Well, time is short and so is my patience. I just wish you the best during your recovery period.

I know it is difficult having your team on the brink of immortality and then having it smashed by Alabama. But I suggest this can be a learning experience for you.

I suggest you get a video of the game and watch it a couple of times. Take a look at how your players behaved during the game compared to Alabama's players.

Same for Coach Gene Stallings.

Perhaps you too can learn a little about class. You also might learn about tradition, the kind earned over a century of football, not bought with renegade players and fair-weather and foul-mouthed fans.

Sincerely,

Your Pal Paul

Another of my famed letter columns. I wish the Bear Bryant stamp had been available at the time I mailed this missive.

JULY 17, 1993

Davey Allison's death is a tragedy that touches everyone

Alabamians often are chastised for their devotion to sports. Some academicians have said the state would be a more preferable place to live if less attention were placed on athletics.

This past week, however, we realized again how important athletes and their quests are to Alabamians. Not that the death of Davey Allison was really about sports.

Clearly, it transcended the sport of auto racing. It was about human drama and suffering. It was about the misery and torment a single family has had to endure. It was about life and death.

Perhaps we all learned something in this week of anguish. Often, in the past, I have commented—unfavorably—in this space about the sport of auto racing. One must respect the men who get behind the wheels of these thundering machines.

On the other hand, often, I have aimed my venomous darts at some of the zealots who follow racing. They have been easy targets for a variety of reasons.

Instead of trying to better understand the people and why they love this sport, I have made broad generalizations. Some of my compatriots who regularly cover the sport have repeatedly told me the large majority of fans who follow the sport are good folks. However, those words often have been disregarded in a narrow view of the scene.

During this terribly tragic week, however, I have finally seen what so many have tried to tell me for so long. The vivid scene of pained NASCAR fans weeping over this cataclysmic event had to tug at one's heart.

Of course, not only race fans were touched by Davey Allison's death. It seemed to have a profound effect on nearly everyone.

In Alabama, commentators always seem to find a way to draw a correlation to Paul "Bear" Bryant when a major event has occurred.

Not since that sad week a decade ago has this state responded to a tragedy in such an overwhelming fashion.

The death of Bryant was sad for many reasons. Bryant, however, was not young and had already retired from his brilliant career. Davey had so many miles yet to race. Still, they were both loved by the citizens of this state—and many others—for their goodness and ability to relate to the common man.

Following the death of Bryant, there were many memorials and tributes. There were streets named after him and museums erected in his honor.

Obviously, there will be similar events to honor Allison. However, it is difficult to think of a more fitting tribute than for the Talladega Superspeedway to be renamed the Davey Allison Memorial Superspeedway. It would be a constant reminder to future fans of the extraordinary contribution the young driver made to the sport and to the speedway, where he was the winningest driver.

On a broader scale, Allison's death has been yet another unfortunate event on the local sports scene. So many of the top personalities in our state have fallen in such a short time.

There was the forced resignation of Wimp Sanderson and the trail of tears that accompanied Pat Dye's farewell at Auburn.

The national sports scene also has been beset by tragedies in recent months, such as the death of NASCAR star Alan Kulwicki. We also saw the terrible deaths of both tennis star Arthur Ashe and basketball coach Jim Valvano.

The baseball season opened shortly after two Cleveland Indians pitchers died in a boating accident.

Throughout it all, life goes on. There are triumphs as well, such as Alabama's national championship celebration.

The good times make us all feel accomplished and full of hope. Yet, it is the tragedy of life that brings it all home.

You see Davey Allison dead at 32. Suddenly, no one feels completely safe anymore. Everyone seems vulnerable.

This was, perhaps, the saddest story I have ever covered in sportswriting.

AUGUST 19, 1993

Auburn, where the (cheating) tradition continues

AUBURN—So Auburn is on NCAA probation again. Some things never seem to change.

For many years, Auburn has struggled to achieve the kind of football prominence as its sister-rival, the University of Alabama.

It has come close, but each time the school has neared the crest, the walls have come tumbling down.

But yesterday, the school was again recognized by the NCAA. Albeit, the distinction was dubious.

In handing down the long-awaited verdict, the NCAA identified Auburn as one of only three universities that have been placed on probation six or more times. That may not quite match Alabama's 12 national championships in 100 years of football. But, hey, there are still a couple of years left in this century for Auburn to catch up.

However, with the most recent two-year probation Auburn has matched the number of Alabama's national crowns, that is, in years served in the NCAA jailhouse. Going back to 1956 and including the current sentence, the Tigers will have served 12 years of probation.

No wonder one of the school's battle chants is: Auburn— The tradition continues.

The mood and tenor of the day in Auburn yesterday were predictably somber. Again, this school is being publicly disgraced in the eyes of the world of college athletics.

One more time, Auburn's dirty linen has been exposed for all to see.

Some say the NCAA threw the book at Auburn. That is a matter of opinion. It was tough in certain respects. But it was relatively light in the critical area of scholarship limitations.

However, the NCAA did not go easy on postseason bowl games and television.

Auburn players probably were not going to a postseason bowl game anyway for the next two years (other than the Blue-Gray). But the television sanctions were a ruthless blow.

Prominence and prestige were not the only things to be lost.

Officials estimate Auburn could lose up to $3 million in revenues in the next two years. That goes on top of about $750,000 the school's athletic department spent on legal fees.

Talk about some folks who really earned their money.

The loss of television will send Auburn's already plunging stock to a new low. If a high school player cannot watch a school on the tube, the chance of him attending is seriously affected.

Of course, while some seemed relieved yesterday that Auburn would only go from 25 to 24 scholarships next year, the question might better be: Will Terry Bowden be able to find 24 quality athletes who are remotely interested in joining this battered school?

Throughout the day, Auburn officials and boosters reacted to this decision with disappointment. The people talked about "putting this behind us and moving on."

That is easier said than done.

Sadly, the worst may be about to begin. The nightmare of uncertainty has ended. However, the reality of picking up the ruins has just begun. Terry Bowden, the energetic but inexperienced rookie coach, talked a good game yesterday. That we have come to expect.

However, his already difficult task has just gotten tougher.

He is known as a great motivator. But it will take more than speeches to keep players on board and interested for what should be a very long haul.

One of the most riveting moments yesterday was the presentation of school president William Muse. Although shaken by the events, Muse delivered a stern address about the future of the program.

"If this program is to survive, there can be no more days like this one," Muse said poignantly.

Muse made sense with his sobering words. But remember that Muse is not the first Auburn president to deliver such a speech in times of darkness.

However, for the sake of the Auburn program, it had better be the last.

This column was a throwback to some of my early ones, in terms of nastiness.

AUGUST 21, 1993

Long, dark days ahead for Auburn

So what now for Auburn?

In the wake of NCAA's eviscerating blow Wednesday, several questions have been raised.

Will Auburn slip back to its old cheating ways? Or will it chart a new course for the future, one barren of booster handouts and T-bone steaks for touchdowns?

William Muse, the school president, delivered a trenchant statement Wednesday, declaring the school will abide by the rules. While his countenance was pained and brow fraught with sweat, it should have come as no surprise. This is what school leaders are mandated to say, whether the institution is on probation or has just won the national championship.

But what happens three years from now if Terry Bowden isn't winning? What happens if the losing streak to Alabama nears double digits and the season-ticket sales dwindle? What happens when there no longer is any football money to donate to the library and university morale—because of a second-rate football program—submerges to new depths?

What happens when prominent alumni come together—after years of divisiveness—and proclaim: "It is time to go out and hire a coach who can go out and give us a football team the university can be proud of again?"

That was the predicament in 1981 when Pat Dye arrived and the only things fans asked him was: "How long is it going to take to beat Alabama?"

Dye's infamous answer: "60 minutes."

I doubt that Dye consciously set out to run a dishonest program. But he was so parched for success and ravenous for domination, he probably looked the other way when assistants and boosters laid cash on players.

But so much for the past.

As for the future, perhaps the most chilling aspect of the NCAA probation is that there no longer is room for error.

The next time even a faint scent of aspersion arises on the Plains, the NCAA will come in like a SWAT team at a kidnapping.

The NCAA has said it is unlikely the death penalty ever will be handed down again. However, it would be sorely tempted to change that in Auburn's case.

Muse even delicately broached the subject the other day, saying he would not tolerate any more misconduct in the program. Was Muse signaling he would shut the program down himself before the NCAA even unpacked its bags? Muse seemed to do the Texas two-step when questioned further on the subject.

After all, this is a fairly smart fellow and he knows he has to pander to both the athletic and academic interests of the university to keep his monthly country-club bills paid.

Still, look for this story to continue to unfold in the coming days.

It is difficult to predict the futute of a program under the circumstances. Certainly, the University of Florida survived two scandals in a decade and now is one of the most successful football programs in the nation.

Other schools have followed the same path.

But for every success story, there is an SMU or Oklahoma, great programs of the past that are struggling to return to the glory days.

So can Auburn come back?

It won't be easy.

However, for Auburn to return to greatness, it will take more than words and pained expressions. It will require distinguished leadership and a sense of unity.

Is Muse the man to lead Auburn out of this black night?

Certainly, he has made the changes and sung the right songs. But has he made the right moves?

Muse brought in Mike Lude as athletic director, partly because of his contacts and reputation. It was believed those attributes would help the school in dealing with the NCAA and enable Auburn to hire a big-name football coach.

Obviously, Lude miscarried on both counts.

The hiring of Bowden also was interesting. Bowden is young and energetic and unsullied.

Yet, can Bowden prove to be the right man to rally the football players—and the fans—to believe in Auburn and back it up with their hard-earned dollars?

That drama is about to unfold.

While it is hazardous to make predictions at such an uncertain intersection, the view here is that Auburn is headed for a long journey in the dark and chilly tundra. It will take vision and leadership and the right people to lead the school back to the promised land.

Can it happen?

It is possible. But it will not be easy. The exhaustive journey will take patience on the part of the Auburn people. Perhaps more than anyone dreamed possible.

Three months after this column appeared, Auburn was celebrating a perfect 11-0 season. As usual, I was right on the mark in writing about the demise of the Auburn program.

August 26, 1993

Playing with Chi Chi and Charles

For weeks, I have told myself that it didn't matter. All I have to do is show up and everything will be fine. But as the day moved closer, I found my palms sweating for no apparent reason. My shoulders began to twitch and my heart fluttered.

The situation wasn't helped when friends began to call the day before the event and calmly ask, "Are you nervous?"

My typical macho response to everyone was "no."

Everyone told me that I should be.

The morning before, a close friend, who happens to be a minister, called me, offering spiritual guidance. I cut off the conversation when he began relaying to me odds against another miracle occurring that week.

I even took a golf lesson the day before the Pro-Am. But I could tell there was great concern written on the lines of the professional's face.

Usually, when I have had a lesson, the pro has been full of humor and laughter. This day, I got the impression the wave good-bye was akin to that of the dockmate waving farewell to the captain of the Titanic.

Finally, the big day arrived. My alarm buzzed loudly at 5:30 a.m. To my surprise, I wasn't nervous. I calmly woke up, showered and had breakfast, never even thinking about golf. I must confess thinking about it for a moment when there in the agate page, was the 9:10 paring of the HealthSouth Pro-Am and my name was listed.

The ride out to Greystone was uneventful.

A huge crowd awaited us on the practice tee. When Chi Chi spotted Charles Barkley, he pointed and shouted: "Michael," jokingly confusing him with basketball star Michael Jordan.

As we walked to the first tee, I began to realize how big a deal this was going to be. To my surprise, the most nervous person out there was Barkley.

He was joking and laughing as we posed for pictures on the first tee. But deep down, I could tell he was uptight.

Why should I worry?

After all, why would a guy with a third-world handicap be concerned about playing in front of 8,000 people alongside two of the biggest sports stars in the world?

Finally, the introductions came at the first tee. Up first was Chi Chi Rodriguez. He was followed by Barkley, Dr. Jim Andrews, and Richard Scrushy.

There were two things I didn't have to be concerned about with this group Either having the biggest bank account or the biggest ego. There was enough of the two of those qualities to fill the Gulf of Mexico.

Everybody hit decent first shots. Then, came my turn.

Was I going to spoil the fun and top the ball, or shank it into the crowd?

Finally, it was my time. As I walked up, Barkley started kidding me about Auburn, saying everything would be fine at his school, despite the NCAA probation. Barkley said every time I hit a bad shot, he was going to holler, "War Eagle."

I looked over and pointed at the crush of television camera operators. "Charles, that may be, but at least my bad shots will be shown on television, unlike your football team this fall."

The joke seemed to loosen me up because I nailed my drive about 225 yards down the fairway.

On the second hole, Barkley and I were at it again.

A woman handed me an Auburn cap, which I promptly placed on my head.

Barkley snapped "Take that off, you couldn't even get in Auburn."

I responded "I could have if I'd have the same guy take my ACT (entrance exam) for me that did for you."

The third hole, a 453-yard par four, was really eventful.

Before Chi Chi shot, Dr. Andrews, who is a member at Greystone, politely warned the world-famous golfer about the meandering creek that often gobbles up golf balls that stray to the right side of the fairway.

Chi Chi, usually a cool customer, but who had barely slept the night before because of a late flight, turned to Andrews and said, "Doc, I am a professional golfer. This is my life. And I don't see a creek there. I only think positive thoughts."

Chi Chi walked up to the tee and promptly hit the ball right into the creek.

Barkley topped his ball right into a creek about 20 yards in front of the tees. His reaction could only be described as volcanic. However, the driver he smashed into the ground survived. But only barely. Scrushy hit a shot out of bounds and Andrews followed.

The famous foursome of multimillionaires had not put a ball in play. So what does a hacker like me do?

I pulled out a three-iron, with the intent of gently putting the ball in play. Chi Chi nixed that idea, and I pulled out my driver. To my shock, I hit one of the best drives of my life and ended on the green in two after cranking a three-wood to about 20-feet of the cup.

At one hole, when Andrews knocked a putt well past the hole, Chi Chi responded: "You're going to get a speeding ticket with that putt."

On the eighth hole, I pulled my drive deeply into woods. I watched it closely, as if there were some hope to find it. I looked over to my caddie. Chi Chi walked over and quipped: "Paul, you don't need no caddy to find your drives. You need a troop of Boy Scouts."

One of the highlights of the day came at No. 10, a 178-yard par-3. After Chi Chi's shot, which landed about 25 feet from the green, he began chatting with someone in the gallery.

So he missed my best shot of the day, a three-iron that landed about 10 feet to the left of the hole.

When Chi Chi approached me on the green, he said, "Pards, you here in two?"

Nope Chi Chi. I was there in one, and I was closer to the pin than you. It was a great thrill. I thought I had another chance to topple Chi Chi. On No. 12, at 416-yard par-4, I hit a five-wood from the fairway from 200 yards out to about six feet of the pin. I thought the sucker was going in. After I made my birdie putt, I was planning to do the word dance just like Chi Chi.

Unfortunately, I three-putted from six feet and crawled off the green in complete embarrassment.

Regardless, it was an enchanting day of golf.

Watching the interaction between Chi Chi and Charles and thousands of kids following was so exciting.

"He's a gentle giant," said Chi Chi about Charles. "The commercial he does is a put-on. This man is a real role model."

Chi Chi had a comment about everything.

"I say to Sir Charles this morning, 'If they let you join Greystone, maybe they'll allow a Puerto Rican to join, too.' "

On a personal level, I learned a lot about these great stars and what it is like to play before 8,000 people and clicking cameras.

It was nerve-racking at times. But mostly, it was fun. And a day of golf I will never forget.

It is difficult to write a story moments after playing golf, dripping in sweat and humiliation. However, I was a lot more confident in front of a computer screen than hitting a three-iron into the wind and over water in front of a large crowd.

NOVEMBER 22, 1993

Stallings had look of a rookie

AUBURN—The wildly swinging pendulum of football power in Alabama struck Tide coach Gene Stallings squarely in the head late Saturday afternoon on his way to the Auburn sidelines at Jordan-Hare Stadium. But it's unlikely Stallings felt the blow.

Apparently, Stallings had taken a knock to the head earlier in the game. How else can one explain one of the stupidest coaching decisions in an Alabama-Auburn game since Pat Dye's inexpicable call on fourth down in 1984 when Bo went the wrong way.

One might call Stallings's blunder: "Fourth and Dumb—The Sequel."

Call it whatever you like, but Stallings's bonehead decision played a pivotal role in destroying Alabama's last hope of winning the biggest football game of the season.

With approximately nine minutes left in the game and Auburn leading 15-14, Alabama faced a fourth-and-1 at its own 29-yard line. Rather than punt, Stallings sent fullback Tarrant Lynch up the middle. He was stopped for no gain, and Auburn took over.

The fourth-down play didn't cost Alabama in points, since Auburn also bungled a chance to score on a fourth-down situation of its own. However, it burned up precious minutes of the clock and left a gasping defense in a terrible spot on the field.

That is to take nothing away from Auburn Coach Terry Bowden, whose football team Saturday was everything that Stallings's was not: well-prepared, well-coached, focused, motivated, disciplined, and burning with a desire to win.

Oh, sure, Bowden made miscalculations in the biggest game of his career. But one would expect that from a young man who 52 weeks ago was trying to beat UAB and Miles for high school recruits. You don't expect mistakes from a coach whose fingers are adorned with national championship and Super Bowl rings.

Stallings and his minions have tried to explain the stinging defeat by criticizing the Southeastern Conference officials. Frankly, the officiating was terrible. But how often this season have you seen a proficient SEC officiating crew?

However, can one blame the zebras for a non-call on the most stunning play of the season: the Patrick Nix-to-Frank Sanders fourth-down touchdown pass? But he also might blame his own vaunted defense, once the most feared in the land, for allowing an ice-cold and untested quarterback to strike gold.

Stallings can blame anyone he wants. However, this game looked as if it were his first as a head coach in Tuscaloosa instead of his 48th.

On the other side, what else can be said about Bowden and the job his staff did this football season?

Many people shook their heads when Bowden announced that Wayne Hall would be retained as defensive coordinator.

However, Bowden turned Hall loose, and the former Alabama player did a splendid job. Bowden's biggest concern now will be keeping Hall at Auburn. Undoubtedly, there will be plenty of suitors for a coach with his genius.

Something also must be said about the Auburn people. They threw one of the greatest football parties ever witnessed in this state. The campus was electrified, as was the scene at the stadium.

The spirit of the Auburn people all year—and especially Saturday—played a monumental role in pushing the team forward during this dream season.

Auburn people could have lost hope after the NCAA lowered the boom back in August. That would have been easy and predictable. Instead, they maintained that the sun would come out tomorrow. It did. Saturday, it burned brighter at Jordan-Hare Stadium than one could ever remember.

So what now?

Auburn must sit back and watch as the bizarre and ever-changing national championship race unfolds. Should Auburn win the title? Is it worthy?

That is matter of debate, but Auburn has done everything possible to be considered. It is the best team in the SEC.

Forget what Bill Curry says about Tennessee. Auburn has cudgeled every SEC opponent on the schedule. Therefore, it is the best. End of argument.

Auburn now can relax and enjoy the sweet fruits of victory as SEC commissioner Roy Kramer—with hands over cheeks that should be crimson from embarrassment—must try to promote his championship game with a straight face.

For Alabama, the questions are only beginning.

Will it have anything left for Florida in the SEC championship game? If so, does it really matter?

Stallings has some soul-searching to do. He can continue to mention how few losses he has had over the past few years. However, it seems each time he brings this up, he is adding another defeat to the ledger.

Alabama's fall from the mountain has been excruciating. Of course, there are many reasons, including a rash of injuries. However, that is part of football.

So the usual post-Alabama-Auburn-game soul-searching has begun, as it always does this time of year. But the conclusion is rather simple. Right now, Bowden is the hottest and brightest star in the coaching galaxy.

the past doesn't matter very much in the present. While many people celebrated the national championship last winter and scoffed at the Bowden hiring, the Auburn program was roaring back.

Saturday afternoon, in the splendiferous setting of Jordan-Hare Stadium, Bowden and his Tigers left Stallings and the wounded pride of the Crimson Tide in their tracks.

I guess after this column, it was no surprise that Gene Stallings took me off his Christmas card list. Naturally, I had predicted Alabama to win this game. Naturally, I was wrong.

April 25, 1994

Nixon's trick was always bouncing back

Two thousand years ago, the eminent poet Sophocles wrote, "One must wait until the evening to see how splendid the day has been." The epigram was one of Richard M. Nixon's favorite sayings. And how propitious it was that Sophocles's writings were heeded and that Nixon's life wasn't completely judged until twilight.

Since Nixon's death Friday evening, I have been unable to get him off my mind. Each time I attempted to force the subject of today's column to sports, whether it be Michael Jordan's success in baseball or spring football or the NFL draft, my mind kept drifting back to Nixon.

I was not a great supporter of Nixon. At the time of his last election, in 1972, I wasn't old enough to vote. Although, I did proudly display a bumper sticker in my room at home at the time, proclaiming: "Don't Blame Me, I Voted for McGovern."

Regardless, Nixon has been the seminal political figure of my life, and one who has had a profound effect on both my career and and the profession of journalism.

It was during the Watergate hearings that my voracity for journalism sharpened. I listened to the doublespeak of Nixon's aides and wanted to be there myself, firing off questions. I read the writings of Bob Woodward and Carl Bernstein and lived vicariously through their work.

The era of Watergate also changed journalism. A new breed of hungry reporters, all trying to make a name for themselves like the aforementioned, parachuted out of journalism schools with dreams of grandeur.

They all wanted to be the next Woodward and Bernstein. Unfortunately, there never has been another Watergate, although the news media have tried to turn almost every major scandal since then into it.

There was IranGate and now White Watergate.

And in sports, the Eric Ramsey story was dubbed by a certain columnist (blush!) "Ramseygate."

That same fellow, who will decline to be identified but who clearly is preoccupied by Nixonian comparisons, also has described the case involving Gene Jelks as Jelksgate.

During the final days of Pat Dye's reign at Auburn, I seriously considered doing a comparison between the two men and the similarity of their falls.

How were they analogous?

For starters, both grew up poor and fought hard to overcome the class system of this nation. Both enjoyed great success, followed quickly by cataclysmic defeats.

The two men's careers were both brought down to shattering halts by tape recordings. Both men hung on to their jobs long after any realistic hope of surviving.

Interestingly, the president and the former Auburn coach named their books with identical titles.

Nixon's political memoir, published in 1990, was titled *In the Arena*.

Dye's autobiography, published in 1992, was also titled *In the Arena*.

I asked Dye about this once.

"If I would have known, I would have changed the name," he said.

The men always took the role of the underdog, often striking back at the media for their own faults.

The Nixon White House described the Watergate break-in as a "third-rate burglary."

Asked about the "60 Minutes" broadcast, which helped lead to his resignation, Dye responded: "What did Mr. Shakespeare say? A lot of sound and fury signifying nothing."

I will miss Richard Nixon. He was a great sportsman, from his clumsy play he gave George Allen in the 1973 Super Bowl to his love of baseball. It was said Nixon would have gladly accepted the commissionership of baseball. I think he would have been good.

He will be remembered for many things, from his foreign policy accomplishments to his Watergate blunder. But I will always remember him for something he said at his farewell speech at the White House.

Nixon talked about Teddy Roosevelt's coming back from defeat and said he used the words in his own career.

They are words worth reading and remembering.

"We think that when someone dear to us dies, we think that we lose an election, we think that when we suffer a defeat, that all is ended. We think, as T. R. said, that the light has left his life forever.

"Not true. It is only a beginning, always. The young must know it; the old must know it. It must always sustain us, because the greatness comes not when things go always good for you, but the greatness comes and you are really tested when you take some knocks, some disappointments, when sadness comes, because only if you have been in the deepest valley can you ever know how magnificent it is to be on the highest mountain.

"Always give your best, never get discouraged, never be petty; always remember, others may hate you, but those who hate you don't win unless you hate them, and then you destroy yourself."

I don't think I helped my relationship with Pat Dye by comparing him to Nixon. On second thought, who cares?

JUNE 22, 1994

Talent does not create heroes

On the television screen, the words and pictures told the story.

"Coming up next, we'll have the latest on O. J. Simpson, the fall of an American hero."

That theme has been repeated since the news first broke about the former Heisman Trophy winner. As a nation, we throw up our hands, raise our eyes, and feign shock and dismay.

"Say it ain't so, O. J.," resonates throughout the land.

The spoiling of a sports icon almost has become the norm instead of the exception in our nation. In case you haven't been paying attention—as most sports fans prefer to do—look the other way, there is a long list of so-called sports heroes who have crashed and burned.

Five years ago, there was the soiled saga of Pete Rose, followed quickly by Mike Tyson. And there are countless other thugs who pervade the world of sports, such as Vince Coleman, Darryl Strawberry and Tonya Harding.

This is quite a collection of sport idols. It's about time the public realizes these people are nothing but riffraff. Perhaps it is wrong to paint with such a broad brush. But professional sports heroes generally are a spoiled-rotten, nasty group of over-aged children who usually get their way, regardless of whether their actions fall within the laws governing the land. The time has come for the public and the news media to quit making them something they are not.

O. J. Simpson is not an American hero. Instead, he was an astonishingly talented running back—arguably the best of all time—who also was a complete buffoon on television and in the movies.

Some people have said O. J. was a fine actor. But I never thought the Juice was acting by playing the idiotic stooge of a police officer in the "Naked Gun" trilogy.

As a television sportscaster, he was like many other former athletes turned commentators: inarticulate, garbled, at times incomprehensible and annoying (and not necessarily in that order).

ABC fired him as one of three commentators on "Monday Night Football," much to the relief of the nation. With O. J. reporting a game, one often needed a United Nations interpreter to fathom what he was attempting to say.

On the television screen in recent years for NBC Sports, he always was one of the boys, laughing and joking with his buddies on the field, doing no real reporting and usually apologizing.

Perhaps that is why O. J. has garnered so much sympathy from the sports world.

But overlooked in all of this was Simpson's 1989 plea of no contest to spousal abuse. His friends in the sports world looked the other way probably using the age-old axiom of good-ol' boys: "She probably deserved it."

Obviously the judge in the case must have thought the same thing. Had O. J. been forced to serve time, perhaps Nicole Brown Simpson and Ronald Goldman would be alive. Had O. J. Simpson been made to understand that a man cannot severely batter a woman, whether it is his wife or a stranger, he might have paid his debt in full and be walking the streets today, living the good life he so enjoyed and having better understood.

But athletes are spoiled rotten in our society. They are allowed to enter restaurants through the back door instead of waiting in line out front. They are glorified and idolized by the public and, sadly, by the news media because they can run a football or dunk a basketball.

Many athletes give back to the community. Michael Jordan has raised countless millions for charity through his name and time. I'm sure O. J. did the same.

But something went wrong. Because O. J. could run a football better than anyone else he was able to profit handsomely.

However, as fast as O. J. could run on the football field or through a crowed airport he was not able to outrun the law.

One must presume his innocence until further notice. Who knows? In Los Angeles, it seems almost anyone can get off for practically anything. Hitler probably could have beaten a rap, given the demented state of the community.

Behind that, hopefully, we will learn a lesson from the O. J. Simpson story.

Perhaps we the people can send a message to so-called sports heroes by treating them the same way they treat us. Perhaps then, and only then, can a lesson be learned and tragedies avoided.

So what is the real lesson learned from O. J. Simpson? On a personal note, I learned that I would have been better off dropping this ridiculous project and getting an O. J. Simpson book on the shelves. While this book is gathering dust on the discount rack, the stuff on O. J. is selling like hotcakes. Have you ever wondered why hotcakes sell so fast?

To be continued...